new directions

new

FOR
HIGHER
EDUCATION

number 1
spring 1973

new directions for higher education

a quarterly sourcebook edited by
JB Lon Hefferlin

number 1
spring 1973

facilitating
faculty
development

mervin freedman
issue editor

Jossey-Bass Inc., Publishers
San Francisco • Washington • London

FACILITATING FACULTY DEVELOPMENT
New Directions for Higher Education
Volume I, Number 1, Spring 1973
      Mervin Freedman, Issue Editor

New Directions for Higher Education is published quarterly
by Jossey-Bass, Inc., Publishers. Subscriptions are available
at the regular rate for institutions, libraries, and agencies
of $25 for one year. Individuals may subscribe at the special
professional rate of $15 for one year. Application to mail at
second-class postage rates is pending at San Francisco, California,
and at additional mailing offices.

Correspondence:
Subscriptions, single-issue orders, change of address notices,
undelivered copies, and other correspondence should be sent to
New Directions Subscriptions, Jossey-Bass, Inc., Publishers,
615 Montgomery Street, San Francisco, California 94111.
Editorial correspondence should be sent to the Editor-in-Chief,
JB Lon Hefferlin, at the same address.

Library of Congress Catalogue Card Number LC 73-2589

Cover design by Willi Baum
Manufactured in the United States of America

contents

a welcome

Arnold Toynbee begins *A Study of History* with the observation that during his lifetime periodicals had overrun books. As a child he had noticed that the library shelves of a friend were filled with wide-ranging volumes on literature and science, but "as the years passed, these shelves were invaded, one after another, by the relentless advance of half a dozen specialized periodicals—gaunt volumes in grim bindings, each containing many monographs by different hands." Among these journals, Toynbee recalls, "there was no unity in their contents and indeed no relation whatever between one monograph and another beyond the very feeble link of their all having something to do with the branch of science in question"; and he observes that while the books retreated and the periodicals advanced, "each time I found the study a less agreeable room to look at and to live in than before."*

Now, in an age of print pollution, when the gaunt periodicals in grim bindings have not only filled library shelves but inundated desks, chairs, and windowsills of offices and studies, we are inaugurating a series of volumes that attempt to bridge the gap between these journals with no unity in their contents and scholarly books and monographs by single authors.

New Directions for Higher Education is a series of topical sourcebooks, with each quarterly issue designed to provide compact yet comprehensive information about a pressing educational problem. Through a synthesis of recent research and realistic suggestions from experts on the problem, it aims to indicate new options, new possibilities, and new directions for the academic community. We will try to make it useful, not pedantic; informative, not obscure; and of more benefit and enjoyment than the periodicals Toynbee found so disagreeable and others find so discontenting.

This inaugural issue contains the findings and recommendations of Mervin Freedman and other scholars who in recent years have been seeking to help colleges and universities promote the

---

*Arnold J. Toynbee, *A Study of History*, second edition, volume I (London: Oxford University Press, 1951), p. 2.

personal and professional growth of their faculty members. In 1967 Freedman and Joseph Axelrod helped inaugurate the Jossey-Bass series of professional books in higher education as its editors and developed it into a widely recognized resource for new knowledge about higher education. They have honored *New Directions for Higher Education* by participating in the first issue of what we hope will become an equally useful aid for colleges and universities.

J B Lon Hefferlin
Editor-in-Chief

By development I mean a heightening of self-awareness, an increase of autonomy, and a broadening of perspective on the world. My concern is that faculty better understand themselves and their social and organizational situation, and my hope is that such knowledge will make them better teachers, better researchers, better educators generally.

This use of the term *development* is different from the conventional meanings it has acquired in recent decades. Most programs of faculty development—orientation sessions, sabbaticals, visiting lecturers, and the rest—are designed primarily to help professors be more effective in their present professional roles. For example, leaves from teaching and other customary duties most often have the object of enabling faculty to do more research in their special domain.

There is, of course, some benefit from faculty members being better adjusted, happier, and more efficient in their professional roles, but being in these very roles as they are now defined can foster narrow outlooks and impair the realization of human potentialities. More than that, there are needs in higher education in the United States today that transcend smooth adjustment or efficient functioning in the existing academic structure. The system of higher education, as we have known it for a century in this country, may be dying; certainly it is being radically transformed. True educational leadership is hard to find. In the past few critical years most leadership has come from politicians, government functionaries, officers of foundations, and comparable external figures. It is high time for faculty to assert themselves responsibly in educational debate and planning.

"Facilitating Faculty Development" is dedicated to the proposition that heightened understanding of themselves and their social and organizational situation will enable faculty members to assume their rightful place as educational leaders on their own campuses, as well as on the national scene. The topic stems from an interest that many of us who worked on *The American College* a decade ago have shared in the intervening years—an interest in trying to understand the development of faculty members in the same detail with which that volume analyzed the development of students.

Five years ago my colleagues and I at the Wright Institute began an intensive research program on faculty growth and development, with assistance from the United States Office of Education, Grant OEG-9-70-0035(057). Since then we have conducted lengthy interviews with some five hundred randomly selected professors on campuses as diverse as Central Michigan University and Stanford, Johnston College at the University of Redlands, and the University of California, Berkeley. In a forthcoming book edited by Wesley Brown, Robert Shukraft, and myself, we will report in detail on this research. In this issue of *New Directions for Higher Education,* three of my colleagues in this project—Nevitt Sanford, Michael Bloom, and Norbert Ralph—and I have developed, with the assistance of a grant from the Lilly Endowment, some of the implications of this research for institutional practice.

We have asked three other colleagues from other institutions to share their experience as well: Joseph Axelrod, who has developed several new concepts of the faculty member's role as a result of his own recent research at the Center for Research and Development in Higher Education; Donald R. Gerth, who has been developing a faculty facilitation program at California State College, Chico; and John F. Noonan, who has been similarly active at Findlay College.

All in all, we present psychological, social psychological, and sociological perspectives on the situation of faculty. We conclude that the time is long past when colleges and universities, and faculty members themselves, could think of faculty as finished products. Academic institutions must be as concerned with the development of their faculty as with the development of their students and must provide educational opportunities for faculty to understand themselves better.

Academic men and women have been slow to study themselves and their habitat. If this issue of *New Directions for Higher Education* stimulates some faculty members to take a penetrating look at themselves and some administrators to help them do so, we shall consider our efforts a success.

Mervin Freedman
Editor

*Changes in higher education have markedly
increased faculty anxiety and uncertainty in
the past two years and made improvements
in faculty development programs urgent.*

the faculty member yesterday and today

mervin freedman
nevitt sanford

Between the end of the nineteenth century and 1965 the situation
of American college and university faculty members changed but
little. They lectured to undergraduate students, conducted seminars
with graduate students, and advised and counseled students at both
levels. In some institutions, mainly the prestigious universities, they
engaged in research. Despite the antiintellectualism endemic to certain strata of American society they enjoyed considerable prestige
in the larger community. Students were usually polite. If they
shared but little in the life of the mind or culture, they found their
pleasures elsewhere and did not trouble their professors. After
World War II college attendance became an integral part of the
American way of life. Faculty positions were plentiful, and, particularly in the late 1950s and early 1960s, salaries rose rapidly.

All this is now changed. Faculty positions are scarce, and
money is in short supply. Faculty members are enjoined to do more
socially useful research or to eschew research entirely. They are

1

urged to teach more students and more classes and to teach in different and more effective ways. The Free Speech Movement at the University of California and subsequent student rebellions shattered the era of good feeling for faculty members. Students are often contrary, sometimes downright hostile. The system of higher education, which formerly rivaled the military in organization and precision, now resembles an exploding galaxy. Open admissions, "less time-more options," "universities without walls," and alternative educational programs are prominent features of the educational scene, receiving encouragement and support from prestigious foundations and federal, state, and local governments.

The situation of higher education has thus become highly unpredictable. Whereas Clark Kerr in *The Uses of the University* (1962) depicted the multiversity as an institution destined to cast a long shadow over the American landscape for a millenium and Christopher Jencks and David Riesman in *The Academic Revolution* (1968) detailed the hegemony of academic disciplines and departments, the perspective of 1973 suggests that the multiversity may well be in trouble—if not actually struggling for its very survival—and the dominance of disciplines and departments over colleges and universities and even over the organization of knowledge faces serious challenges. This is not to say that traditional academic ways and structures are done, or even on the way out. History tells us that such social forms tend to have great persistence despite surface alterations. At least for a while, however, higher education will be a curious and uneasy melange of the old and the new, the traditional and the unconventional, the highly structured and the highly flexible.

The life of the faculty member today, then, is not easy—not as easy, at any rate, as it used to be. The well-trodden paths and the signposts that directed his or her professional ways have become blurred and in some cases obliterated. Tradition, custom, and convention no longer serve to organize his life. A young faculty member must forge his own role, and many an older faculty member must fix a level gaze on the beliefs and activities of decades. This experience may be an exciting challenge, but it is likely to be trying as well. In all events there is no way around it. Faculty members have no choice but to examine themselves and their social and professional situation. They can attain control over their professional lives and the society and organizations in which they live only to the degree that they can understand what is happening to them and to the world they inhabit.

faculty attitudes and faculty development

In the past three years our colleagues and we at the Wright Institute have interviewed more than five hundred faculty members at a wide variety of institutions ranging from large, research-oriented universities to more or less invisible liberal arts colleges. These interviews, averaging about two hours in length, covered a lot of ground—the faculty member's personal and intellectual history, his education, his attitudes toward students and teaching, his feelings about his institution, and his opinions of the state of his discipline. In these interviews, we found among academic men and women a pervasive unease and confusion and, most strikingly, a lack of professional identity. They do not seem to have a sense of belonging to a body of professionals with shared goals, shared procedures for attaining them, and agreed ways of estimating their realization. In the area of published research we found some agreement concerning proper performance and evaluation but this consensus is small comfort to the majority of faculty members who do not publish or even do any scholarly research beyond their Ph.D. dissertations. Most faculty members have little sense of their impact on students, beyond some formal knowledge of how much content students learn. Even if they perceive that they are not teaching well, they probably do not know how to be more effective. Higher education has virtually no pedagogy, and without it no rational system of rewards for good teaching can be put into practice. And most faculty members have only the vaguest idea of the organizational workings or the social psychology of their institution. Frequently, therefore, they are the victims of stupid and callous educational and organizational policy.

Our objective is the development of faculty members. By development we mean favorable change whose consequence is that faculty members operate with increasing autonomy in accord with internalized values and goals—and function more effectively as individuals and as members of society. Greater understanding of themselves and of their social surroundings can promote such development. They need some sense of the kinds of past experiences that have led to the careers they have chosen. They need to know how they have been influenced by graduate school, by socialization in their discipline, and by faculty culture. They need some understanding of personal development in the adult years. They need insight into the forces of society at large and those of their colleges and universities that impinge directly upon them.

In writing about faculty development we seek to foster conceptions of professors as highly complex individuals. Narrow conceptions of faculty and their activities have probably been the chief barrier to improved education and teaching. Administrative reorganization of educational priorities will have little or no impact—except to sow discontent and discord—unless such planning is based on enlarged awareness of faculty members and their situation. Similarly, programs designed to reward "good" teaching, render assistance to poor teachers, or train "good" teachers will surely founder unless they are based on such understanding of faculty members.

the myth of the golden past versus the master plan

Implicit in the vision of the academic community held by most faculty is Plato's Academy—a group of intellectuals sitting around the agora or in a garden sipping wine and holding forth in sparkling conversation. This vision has shaped the education of graduate students, at least until recently. Implicitly, they are socialized to enter a disembodied intellectual life in which politics has no place.

The realities of academic life are, of course, very different. Ideologies and social forces strongly influence scholarship. Veblen's mordant critique of higher education may have oversimplified matters, but its political accuracy is indisputable. Prior to World War II the entrance of Jews into academic life was consistently restricted. Until recently blacks, Chicanos, and other racial or ethnic minorities—and women—faced the same exclusion. Some faculty members have pursued wealth and power, just like politicians, industrialists, and other professional men. Yet the mythology of the faculty member denied the political nature of these activities. In his vision politics was beneath him and did not intersect with true intellectual life. If somehow he was forced to engage in political life, the honorable thing was to withdraw as soon as possible.

In the past this flawed vision was functional enough. In the fairly static academic world of 1900-1965 it often mattered little whether or not faculty members were involved in political matters. A pretty good maxim, in fact, was "The more things change, the more they remain the same." Anyone who has participated in institutional self-studies of the past, curriculum revisions, or the intense debates in faculty meetings knows that it usually made little difference in the long run how one voted. Formal changes of structure and procedure had about as much functional significance as the constitution of the U.S.S.R. After the change was inaugurated, everyone could go on behaving much as he had before.

But again things are different now. State governors, state legislators, the United States Office of Education, trustees, chancellors, and presidents often make decisions that truly matter. A faculty member who still somehow regards politics as beyond the pale is likely to suffer. His world will be governed by leaders or planners who give him little or no consideration. For these "futurists" and global strategists, faculty and students alike are but statistical units. Faculty members are increasingly aware of this state of affairs and they complain about not being consulted, but it hardly occurs to them that they might take the lead. A faculty member who wishes to participate in determining his own fate is likely to be handicapped by his limited appreciation of the forces affecting his own situation and that of his colleagues.

Consider the phenomenon of open admissions. Decisions to inaugurate such a policy are usually based on abstract political or social concerns. Certain political leaders believe that open admissions will benefit their constituents, and certain other individuals who occupy high-status positions consider that admissions reform is long overdue, equitable, and just. But implementation of such policy at the lower levels is almost left to chance. Although some provisions may be made for helping those students who require it, the money and resources necessary to carry out such supportive programs effectively are usually inadequate. Concern among policy-makers about how faculty will be affected by open admissions is almost nil. Grumblings and objections from faculty are considered to be manifestations of their rigidity and conservatism, matched only by the academic conservatives of czarist Russia or nineteenth century France. One simply has to drag them, kicking and screaming, into the 1970s.

Consequently in many places open admissions programs have fared badly—particularly at four-year colleges and universities that previously admitted only "qualified" students. Confused and uncertain, many faculty have been unable to pitch their teaching or standards to the changed background and level of understanding of their classes. They have either failed high proportions of students, or they have grudgingly passed students who in their eyes have learned little. Generally they worry that the natural flow of their teaching and academic lives has been disrupted.

Under these conditions it is no wonder that faculty have sometimes been called racist and elitist. Racism, elitism, and academic conservatism are hardly to be ignored, of course, but it takes little imagination to appreciate that faculty members are not operatives on an assembly line who can be required to carry out mechanically every function that efficient production demands at any given time. As later articles in this issue indicate, faculty members are likely to have their whole beings invested in their work, whether teaching, or research, or both. They have chosen a discipline and a profession to pursue and a kind of institution in which to work because of deep inner needs, and their graduate education and their sense of belonging to a discipline and profession have fostered a tradition of certain roles and functions. While they might benefit personally and professionally by departures from their customary activities, very likely they will need help to do so. One may well argue that open admissions calls for as much attention to the faculty who are to teach the new students as it does to the students themselves.

Various master plans, statewide and others, pose comparable problems. Various institutions are assigned different functions according to statistics—certain numbers of students, certain amounts of money available, certain kinds and numbers of employment opportunities, and the like. On the basis of such information "high-level" functionaries make decisions: these institutions will concentrate on graduate education and research, those on four-year undergraduate education, others on two-year programs, and so forth. Even if the statistics and the predictions concerning future trends are correct—a dubious assumption, indeed—such planning presumes that faculty members represent interchangeable parts of a system. It is supposed, for example, that they can readily forego teaching graduate students for undergraduates if the system demands it. But our interviews indicate that plans which fail to take into account the situation and needs of faculty will probably founder—if not by outright obstructionism, by confusion, incrimination, and antagonism. Faculty members who have been teaching traditional students in traditional ways are not automatically able to teach new kinds of students in other ways. If they are to assume new functions and responsibilities they will need some help. In the absence of such assistance they are likely to cling with a vengeance to traditional ways. In the face of confusion and uncertainty people usually fall back on tried and true methods, because there they find security. So demands on faculty to change their conventional and traditional procedures often result in retrenchment rather than change.

pressures for production

At the same time that teaching is becoming more complex and difficult and faculty are being urged to take teaching more seriously and to do more of it, one hears much of accountability—which often comes down to the number of students taught per year by each faculty member. Class sizes are being increased, and in some states teaching assignments or duties are actually being mandated by the state legislature. Faculty are enjoined to understand students, to be interested in their development, to be "relevant" in their teaching, and are reminded that learning involves more than mastery of the abstract content of a discipline; yet for them to reconcile interest in students and relevant teaching with larger classes and greater diversity among students is a difficult task.

Similarly, faculty are now enjoined to foster more classroom discussion in place of lectures on the assumption that lecturers and discussion leaders are interchangeable. Individuals who may be poorly suited for managing discussions are not helped to improve their techniques. Programs of student evaluation of faculty are instituted without regard for faculty sensibilities, yet faculty members are expected to accept such evaluation with equanimity—even when it is public; indeed, they are expected to welcome it. The fact is, however, that most faculty members cannot assimilate such criticism, no matter how much they might benefit from it. Teaching is a highly personal matter, and criticism of one's effort is experienced and resisted as a direct attack on one's self. Hence most systems of student evaluation of faculty or teaching become *pro forma* rituals that allow all participants in the procedure to go on behaving as they always have. And although various programs designed to produce good teachers have been instituted in recent years—doctoral programs emphasizing more than research, for example—in the absence of a pedagogy of higher education, it is difficult to be sanguine about these endeavors. They seem to be founded on the faith that practice has beneficial outcomes even if we do not know what we are doing. Yet in a more limited sense, it probably is true that practice reduces anxiety and increases assurance, thereby contributing to effective teaching.

a pedagogy of higher education

The flood of literature on colleges that appeared during the turbulent years of the late 1960s illustrates very well the meagreness of thought concerning higher educational matters. Almost nothing in that body of literature—defending, attacking, or impartially analyzing faculty, administrators, and rebellious students—has stood the test of just a few years' time. The reason why there is so little present interest in this writing is its lack of any theoretical base. Almost none of it was tied to theories of teaching and learning, of faculty and student development, or of the workings of educational institutions. Instead it was topical, transitory, ephemeral.

Educational researchers have not entirely neglected the subject of college teachers and teaching, although Sanford's *The American College* (1962) noted the paucity of research on higher education compared with studies of elementary and secondary school teaching, and most inquiries have been directed toward relatively superficial aspects of "how to do it" rather than toward attitudes, values, and ways of conceiving the teacher's role and functions. Gage's comprehensive handbook on teaching, for example (1963), contains an authoritative chapter on college teaching by W. McKeachie, but McKeachie's views on attitudes and values are necessarily based only on his impressions; he can cite no research on this topic, even though his bibliography for the chapter as a whole is massive.

Basic aspects of teaching in higher education—lecturing, leading discussions, and advising students, for example—have barely been touched by systematic inquiry. In this issue Axelrod offers a new classification of these instructional activities, but the skills and personal qualities that engender success in one of these endeavors

may not hold for others, just as the training that faculty may re
quire to become proficient in these activities will vary from person
to person.

There has also been a lack of systematic information on the
relation of teaching to subject matter. Certain teaching procedures
may well be more effective in the physical sciences than in the
social sciences. Discussions of the roles of women in Western society, race relations, or sexual development are likely to evoke more
emotional or high-energy interchanges in comparison with discussions of transportation problems, Restoration drama, or the nature
of language. And what factors affect students' behavior? The hostility, inertia, or enthusiasm they exhibit in class is not entirely a
function of any one course. It may reflect the state of student
morale in the institution or the national situation of youth.

teachers and students

Faculty and students are joined in a very complex system,
and our interviews indicate that faculty members are much influenced by the attitudes and reactions of their students, undergraduate or graduate. It is a rare faculty member, even at a prestigious
research university, who proclaims that research is his chief academic interest and that students matter little to him. Most faculty
members are interested in their teaching and believe they are doing
at least an adequate job, but recent years have brought uncertainty
about their relations to students.

It may be, in fact, that traditional liberal education has
reached a dead end. Since World War I a very important element of
liberal education—perhaps its most exciting quality—has been its
attempt to introduce a sense of openness and relativism in students'
minds. In college, students have learned that official American actions have not always held up well under moral scrutiny; that all
virtue does not reside in Christianity, or Protestantism, or Episco-
palianism; that conventional morality is a dubious set of beliefs;
that virtue is not always rewarded; and so on. These were exciting
revelations when most freshmen were constricted and authoritarian
(as they still are on many campuses), and faculty who provided
them were exciting figures. The views of graduating seniors represented something of a compromise between the complex outlook,
relativism, and sophistication of faculty, on the one hand, and the

more traditional or conventional outlook of home environment and family on the other.

These days, however, freshmen on some campuses are more relativistic than their faculty. They are familiar with political demonstrations and with arrests for use of illegal drugs. Traditional patriotism has been eroded by years of criticism of the war in Vietnam. G. B. Shaw and D. H. Lawrence are not shockingly liberating, as once they were, to young people who have read the underground press or Eldridge Cleaver in high school. In the past, faculty liberals were in an enviable position—they could side with their students against prudery, conventionality, reactionary public figures, and outmoded laws—but now their situation is more complex. Often they find themselves in the unaccustomed role of allying with exponents of law and order.

In the complacent, quiescent Eisenhower era, we and several colleagues studied personality development among college students. One product of our researches was the Developmental Status Scale (Webster, 1958), which measured, among various traits, critical attitudes toward authority—"rebellious independence," as we called it. At almost every college or university where this scale has been administered, seniors score significantly higher than freshmen. Even in the 1950s, when faculty members were chastising students for their complacency and "privatism," rebellious independence was mounting during the college years. Not only did it increase between the freshman and senior years, but each successive freshman class— at most institutions that we studied—was likely to have a higher score than its predecessor. Whatever its historical origins, the growth of rebellious independence among students over the last two decades may be documented empirically. Each autumn many colleges and universities admit freshman classes that show less deference toward authority of all kinds—the family, the church, the state, the school—than did their predecessors.

As regard for authority wanes, diversity of opinion and outlook on the campus increases. One may find student exponents of Maoism, Gay Liberation, Black Liberation, Women's Liberation, and psychedelic drugs, as well as a range of more traditional social and political views. And students are usually not loathe to express their sentiments. In such fields as mathematics and physical science, hostile student opinion may not be of major moment, although from time to time a physicist may be denounced for serving the forces of imperialism or exploitative capitalism. In the social sciences and the humanities, however, faculty members may frequently encounter students who are not humble in expressing their disapproval or dissatisfaction. In the course of our interviews we talked to a number of faculty members who plan to retire early because their teaching experiences have become difficult if not actually unpleasant. Some of them had formerly enjoyed their teaching duties, but as a man in a physical science told us: "I plan to retire in three years at age fifty-five. I don't seem to understand students any more, and they don't seem to understand me. They don't seem interested in what I have to say. I find them impolite. They don't work as hard as they used to. I suppose I'm old-fashioned. I liked students better in the past."

faculty culture

A traditional faculty orientation cannot help this professor adjust to changes in students and society. Instead of a profession geared to continued development, college and university professors have a kind of "culture"—a set of shared ways and views designed to make their ills bearable and to contain their anxieties and uncertainties. Perhaps the clearest evidence that teaching undergraduates is not a true profession is the fact that professors, when they talk shop, almost never discuss their teaching. Nor do they discuss philosophy of education in an abstract way. This is not surprising, for teaching and philosophy of education are subjects in which they have little background. Discussions of educational programs or reforms usually proceed as if education had no discipline, no organized or systematic body of theory and knowledge, and no need for such a discipline. In short, faculty approach teaching and education as would any intelligent adult chosen at random—on the basis of some opinion and reading and some knowledge based on experience.

Thus, although the idea that college and university professors do not like to teach and that they neglect their teaching duties is largely wrong, very few of the faculty members we interviewed could define the basis on which they evaluated themselves or offer any rationale for what they did in the classroom. It was apparent that most of them carried on in the way they had learned as students. Not only does traditional academic culture ignore basic educational issues, it does not even possess the concepts necessary to address them. With no concepts for describing student development, without means to evaluate one's teaching, without even a perspective from which the student may be seen as a person, the professor is denied the most elementary satisfaction of professional activity—seeing desirable things happen as a result of planned action. Moreover, a bureaucratic "unconscious" seems to be more powerful than a personal "unconscious." The chances are that the faculty member can discuss with considerable insight the circumstances of family and personal history that made him what he is today, while he finds it almost impossible to conceptualize how and why decisions are made in his department.

All in all, faculty culture is a fairly grim affair, and it is becoming increasingly so. Research and scholarly activity are frequently harshly competitive. Tenure and promotion structures pit faculty colleagues one against another, and the race is to the swift and strong. Rarely do faculty members have opportunities to work cooperatively; most teaching is an individual and solitary process. Even when the heights have been scaled—that is, when tenure has been attained—faculty members at distinguished institutions are no happier than faculty at "lesser" institutions (Bess, 1970).

Perhaps the most effective argument for faculty members' giving some attention to their own situation and development at this time is the prospect that they might be at least a little happier as a result.

the age of anxiety

Great poets, writers, and artists can feel and express the changes that are taking place in the minds and hearts of men long before others are aware of them. Just as Blake foretold that Newton and mechanistic science would destroy the age-old myths on which Christianity and Western civilization rested, Melville saw that puritanism and Victorianism combined with rationalism, science, and industry would produce in the "suffering depths of the mind . . . a breeding ground of elemental resentments, of an all embracing hostility, and in extreme cases, of nihilism" (Murray, 1953). Eventually, although it may take fifty or a hundred years, these intuitions and insights become widespread among large numbers of men and women. This moment, when a significant change in consciousness occurs, seems to come with a rush. Virginia Woolf describes such an occasion in her penetrating observation that "On or about December 1910 human character changed."

In April 1971 we and our fellow researchers sensed such a moment in the experience of faculty. Between September 1970 and that date we had learned much from some three hundred faculty members about their interest in students, their institutions, their feelings about student unrest, their inability to conceptualize their role as teachers, the sense of some older faculty members that their disciplines were passing them by, and their perceptions of how elected officials, newspapers, magazines, and society at large viewed higher education.

Before April of 1971 their comments about public attitudes hardly captured our imagination—they seemed to be fairly conventional statements of what we rather expected to hear. But one remark of a faculty member-administrator at a respected university, a man of considerable distinction in his field, led us to realize that things had changed. When asked what he expected to be doing ten years hence, he concluded his remarks on his plans to return to teaching, research, and writing with the comment, "That is, if they're still paying us."

None of the previous faculty members, except those in very marginal positions, had said anything like this, but it turned out at the next meeting of our research team that other interviewees were beginning to make similar comments. A sense of vulnerability and threat seemed to be impinging on the consciousness of faculty members that spring, the result, apparently, of many influences— among them, reduced support for higher education by all levels of government; the intervention of government agencies in affairs of colleges and universities ranging from denial of sabbatical leaves to mandated teaching loads; and the growing surplus of doctorates in comparison with available academic positions. Perhaps most pervasive and potent was the sense that the public had grown hostile to academic life and that major elements of society, not just the traditional antiintellectual fringe, were prepared to take political action against higher education.

Nowadays, at three o'clock in the morning an insomniac professor has a lot of external worries in addition to confronting the "deep, dark night of the soul." After listening to the concerns, complaints, fears, uncertainties, and confusions expressed by faculty members in the last two years, one cannot help but wonder: What does all this mean for the future? Is this period but a transient state of upheaval from which colleges and universities will emerge to carry on much as they have for the last century? Or does this expression of anxiety and unease presage the dissolution or radical transformation of one of the major institutions in American society? And if dissolution or transformation is coming, will better forms and structures emerge?

professional self-knowledge

College and university faculty have studied just about every society, culture, and institution under the sun, yet except for a few studies of faculty attitude and opinion, faculty culture and society are practically an uncharted wilderness.

It is, of course, always easier to study other people and other institutions. It took psychoanalysts several decades to recognize that they had to study their own contribution to the process of psychotherapy along with that of their patients. Two centuries after Newton physicists realized that the observer is part of the experimental field and has to take account of both his own whereabouts and the effect of his observations. But faculty opposition to significant study of themselves, their societies and their culture, is powerful and almost universal. The reasons are varied and complex, but it is high time they were explicated, for the need for faculty to understand their professional lives and their institutional situation is now acute. Mobility among young faculty members is declining. No longer can dissatisfied assistant professors presume that they can "go West" and find that paradise that has heretofore eluded them. There is a good chance that they will be spending the next thirty years where they are now. And no longer can all faculty assume that custom and convention will take care of them reasonably well, if they only relax and go with the flow of events. There are too many powerful, and not always benign, social forces at work which would bend universities and their faculties to their will. Now is the time for faculty to bestir themselves and to take the lead in higher education, but they cannot do so unless they understand their professional lives and institutional situation much better than they do now.

15

Bess, J. L. *Patterns of Satisfaction of Organizational Prerequisites and Personal Needs in University Departments of High and Low Quality.* University of California, Berkeley, 1970, unpublished.

Gage, N. L. *Handbook of Research on Teaching.* Chicago: Rand McNally, 1963.

Jencks, C., and Riesman, D. *The Academic Revolution.* Garden City, New York: Doubleday, 1968.

Kerr, C. *The Uses of the University.* Cambridge, Mass.: Harvard University Press, 1963.

McKeachie, W. "Research on Teaching at the College and University Level." In N. L. Gage (Ed.), *Handbook of Research on Teaching.* Chicago: Rand McNally, 1963, pp. 1118-1172.

Murray, H. A. "Conrad Aiken: Poet of Creative Dissolution." *Perspectives U.S.A.*, Fall 1953, No. 5, p. 29.

Sanford, N. (Ed.) *The American College.* New York: Wiley, 1962.

Webster, H. "Changes in Attitudes During College." *Journal of Educational Psychology*, 1958, *49*, 109-117.

Mervin Freedman is professor of psychology, California State University, San Francisco, and dean of the graduate school, The Wright Institute, Berkeley, California. He has been involved in research on higher education for twenty years, since joining Nevitt Sanford at Vassar College to carry out research on student development that led ultimately to The American College. *He has also taught and conducted research at the University of California, Berkeley, and at Stanford, where he served as assistant dean of undergraduate education. Besides contributing to* The American College, *he is the author of* The College Experience *and coauthor of* Search for Relevance. *His current research interests include following up the lives of Vassar students who were interviewed in the 1950s, innovation in graduate education, and the history of the*

psychedelic movement, as well as personality
development in the adult years.
Nevitt Sanford is scientific director of The Wright
Institute, which he founded in 1968 to conduct
research and action programs on consequential
human and social problems. Prior to founding the
Institute he was professor of psychology at
Stanford and director of its Institute for the Study
of Human Problems. He is well known for studies
that eventuated in The Authoritarian Personality
and The American College *and in his more recent*
books Where Colleges Fail, Self and Society,
Sanctions for Evil *(with Craig Comstock and*
associates), and Issues in Personality Theory.
He is particularly interested in the reform of
graduate education, and in developmental education
(as discussed in Sanctions for Evil), *and in the*
study of colleges and universities generally.

New perspective on the roles professors play,
with ideas for the instructor who seeks
to improve his work and for the institution
that seeks to help him do so.

the professor
as artist at teaching

joseph axelrod

Whatever disputes exist among professors who hold different views of teaching, agreement exists on one point: everyone speaks of the *art* of teaching. But if teaching actually is an art, then certain basic questions about it are appropriate. What kind of art, precisely, is teaching? What must a faculty member do to become an artist at teaching? What is the nature of the *artwork* that this particular form of art produces? And how can the college or university professor become more expert at creating this artwork?

The art of teaching, like all other arts, can be studied; it can be observed, discussed, and analyzed, even though its product does not have the permanence and the independent existence that we ordinarily associate with the conventional literary, visual, or musical arts. An artist at teaching can improve—he can move from worse to better as artist—and studying the art should help his development. Teaching in our colleges and universities will improve only as faculty members devote increased attention to the several facets of art involved in teaching, spend some time developing their own aesthetics of teaching, and are encouraged to improve their art by institutional evaluations that recognize legitimate differences of aim and style.

As part of a project which I directed at the Center for Research and Development in Higher Education at the University of California, Berkeley, my staff and I held intensive interviews about teaching with more than a hundred faculty members on a half-dozen campuses. We learned what were the mental images—the "prototypes," as we called them—that professors hold of the ideal university teacher. I will presently describe four prototypes of the teacher-artist, but I would like first to present three limited conceptions of the university teacher that emerged again and again during the course of the interviews. These are unproductive models for building an aesthetics of teaching and I hope the reader will reject them and clear his mind of them as he develops his own philosophy of the teaching art.

The first of these conceptions rests on the metaphor of the teacher as midwife, as the person who helps students give birth to ideas. This metaphor, more than twenty-five hundred years old and still much alive as an image in many professors' minds, derives its power from the myriad connotations and the psychic levels of the birth experience. But if we are looking for a key to the process of artistic creation in teaching, we find the midwife metaphor leading nowhere, for the teacher does more than merely assist the ongoing process of parturition. It is a poor first step for building a systematic aesthetics of teaching.

A second limited conception of the teacher appeared to be especially common among older faculty members. In this view, teaching is a kind of horticultural art: the teacher is seen as a sower of seeds, which sometimes fall on fertile, and sometimes on barren, ground. Popular as it is, this metaphor stops where it starts. For example, as the image is generally envisioned, the sower is never concerned with improving the soil—by adding the nutrients that would render it more fertile—but simply with sowing seeds.

The third common conception is far more grand. Professors who held it were reluctant to express it during our interviews unless they received the right clues from us—sympathetic vibrations—during the conversation. In this conception, the professor is a Jehovah-figure before whom a clod is placed, into which the teacher breathes a soul. This clod is, of course, the college freshman. More university professors see themselves in this role than one might suppose. During our interviews, a professor of English told us that he sees himself playing out the same drama again and again. Among his students, there are some in whom humanness takes shape and motion—mainly because of his efforts, he believes. Inevitably, however, as in *Genesis* and with the same prematurity and secretiveness, these students insist on taking control of their own souls—wherepon these unappreciative creatures are quickly expelled from *his* garden.

None of these conceptions, I am convinced, can contribute anything useful to serious attempts at evolving a clearer understanding of college teaching. But if not these conceptions, what then? Three other conceptions of the professor offer more help: those of the professor as *teacher-craftsman*, as *lecturer-artist*, and as *teacher-artist*.

the teacher as craftsman

Our interviews and class visits showed us how many teachers are excellent craftsmen, working diligently to help students master a body of information or acquire specific skills. In the classes taught by these instructors, inquiry on the part of the student is not required, or even encouraged, in order to complete the learning task: they emphasize a *didactic* mode of teaching in contrast to colleagues who employ what may be called an *evocative* mode of stimulating and encouraging inquiry.

The objectives of teacher-craftsmen are generally clear and relatively easy to formulate. They include the mastery of cognitive knowledge or of verbal, mathematical, or motor-kinetic skills that can be acquired primarily by memorization, repetition, or practice. Our observation of classes falling into this didactic mode included such skills courses as elementary piano, elementary Russian, introduction to logic, beginning photography, freshman English, statistics, algebra, and typewriting. In addition, we observed a number of courses that dealt with substantive issues in the humanities and sciences where students did little more than recite, almost as a catechism, answers to questions about facts and generalizations presented in the textbook. In these classes, no time was devoted to inquiry or, in any significant sense, to weighing alternatives. Indeed, where the teacher's objective is to develop in the student an ability to respond immediately without reflection and where the skills to be acquired do not depend on complex reasoning, the instructor is teaching *against* his aim if he encourages the student to reason out his responses. In such courses, therefore, the ratiocinative processes are kept at a minimum and the teacher-craftsman spends his time in class either giving cues for drills and exercises and correcting the responses he receives from students or posing questions for short-answer recitations and evaluating answers. Or the professor invents artificially simplified problems (or uses ones that are already formulated in textbooks) in order to give students practice in problem-solving. In these courses, the teacher is regarded by all parties as the ultimate authority. Once the student has decided to participate—and he faces penalties if he decides not to—he ordinarily learns there is only one acceptable response to each cue in class or on a written test: the one the professor regards as best.

Many university teachers who thus aim at the acquisition of knowledge and skills are highly effective. This mode of teaching has its own distinctive excellence, and the teacher-craftsman who masters it deserves respect. But the classroom styles of the teacher-craftsman are not the only ones open to university professors. Just as the useful arts are complemented by the fine arts, the didactic skill of the teacher-craftsman is complemented by the evocative art of the teacher-artist.

the professor as lecturer

If we analyze further the art of teaching, we must make a sharp distinction between teaching and another common activity that takes place in the university classroom—that is, lecturing. The relationship between a lecturer and his listeners is vastly different from that which exists between the university teacher and his students.

Although lecturing stands in clear contrast to university teaching, I am not suggesting that students cannot, or do not, learn from it. Nor could I argue that it is not an art. Quite the contrary: it is art of the highest kind. It is, in fact, two arts in one. When the professor who is scheduled to appear before an audience sits down to sketch out or write the lecture he plans to deliver, the act he performs is identical with the act of composing an essay. He is practicing the art of composition. When this professor presents his essay in the university lecture hall, he practices another art, the performing art of oral delivery. The lecturer-artist does not actually know his listeners as students, as individual learners—and he does not, in any significant way, interact with them. His relationship with his audience is akin to that between a television or radio speaker and his listeners, or the relationship that exists between an author and his readers.

Like the teacher-craftsman, the lecturer practices a skill that is difficult to master. It is also an important art: as the university world is now organized, lecturing is one of the most important instructional activities professors engage in. But the art of lecturing is different from the art of teaching. The teacher-artist can be distinguished from the professor who exhibits great talent—or even genius—at university lecturing. Although the teacher-artist may at times use the lecture form, its nature, purpose, and context are quite different from that at which the lecturer is master.

The essential difference between these three types of professors is their relationship with students. This difference will prove crucial in the future development of American higher education. I predict that, by the end of the century, the teacher-craftsman and the lecturer-artist will have become obsolete, while the teacher-artist will have become more and more important in the life of the university. Among all instructional faculty members now working on the university campus, only the teacher-artist will survive.

Startling as such a prediction might appear, it is, in fact, not a very risky one to make. Waiting in the wings are technological developments that will render the teacher-craftsman and the lecturer-artist unnecessary. These developments include products that roll off the printing press; that emerge from radio, tape-player, and television set; that are screened or printed out by the computer as the student engages it in dialogue. It is true that, thus far, only the printing press has yielded products that we have been able to develop into widely used instructional instruments. But as these other "software" products improve and as teachers learn more about their potential and applications—the promise of computer instruction, for example, is especially exciting—they will take the place of the teacher-craftsman and lecturer-artist. Just when this will happen is difficult to say. Predictions about educational technology in the past have been unrealistically optimistic, and I do not expect that important developments along these lines will occur during the next decade. But their effect will certainly be felt quite strongly by the end of the twentieth century. The teacher-artist will survive these developments—continuing to operate very much as he does at the present time—because his relationships with students are, in their very nature, different from the relationships that can be established with nonhuman "instructors."

the teacher as artist

The evocative modes of the artist at teaching differ from the didactic modes of the teacher-craftsman in the emphasis the former give to the process of joint inquiry and discovery by teacher and students. And unlike the lecturer, the artist at teaching seeks to interact actively with his students rather than present a performance to a listening audience. The artworks that he and his students create fall in the category of improvisational art.

The great discussions in which Socrates and his intimates participated as they explored problems together were major works of art and, like the class sessions which the teacher-artist and his students create, they also belong to the category of improvisational art. Since Socrates has traditionally been regarded as the greatest teacher-figure in Western civilization, it is unfortunate that products of his art are not available to us. But they came only fleetingly into existence as Socrates and his colleagues created them and no one, since then, has been able to reexperience them. However, Plato's writings and indirect evidence from other first-hand witnesses enable us to make three observations about Socrates' art—and these apply also to the work of any artist at teaching:

●   First, it is not enough to say that the products of Socrates' art were evanescent. One must add that in Socrates' conception of the teacher's art, such products must always *necessarily* be so.

●   Second, what we know of Socrates' art emphasizes the improvisational nature of the artwork the teacher creates. Neither Socrates nor those with whom he carried on inquiry could predict, when a conversation began, how or where it would go. They did not know in advance what they would discover as they engaged in dialogue or how and when the discoveries would appear. They no doubt anticipated certain probabilities—and such anticipations account, in part, for the pleasure derived from improvisation—but they derived even greater pleasure from perceiving in retrospect that certain developments in the discussion were inevitable, though they came as total surprises.

• Third, the artwork was not created by Socrates alone, although he was surely the master and leader in the group. It was created jointly by him and by every member of the group who entered into a relationship with him during the discussion. It is just that relationship that was crucial. More than any other factor, it determined the kind and the quality of the artwork that emerged.

This third observation about the Socratic art illustrates an important principle about the teaching art in general: all members of the teaching-learning group, and not its leader alone, must become artists if an artwork is to come into existence. This is not to say that there is no difference between the contributions of the leader and the group members. Unlike the leader, other members of the group generally do not know they are creating art. The pleasures and excitement they experience during the session, it is true, come from their participation in the creation of art—inquiring, defining, exploring, discovering, accepting and rejecting, being turned on or off, sometimes laughing and playing with words and concepts —but they are like a primitive dancer who, although his art may be of the highest quality, knows only that he is moving his body without recognizing that these body movements are "art." Yet if the teacher is unable to engage his students in the creative process, he will fail as teacher-artist.

differences among teacher-artists

Our interviews with faculty members whom we identified as teacher-artists revealed that they held several different conceptions of their role, depending on the importance they attributed to each of the three component elements of the teaching-learning process: the subject matter being taught, the teacher, and the learner. Typically, professors emphasize one or another of these elements and expect the other two to accommodate themselves to its demands and requirements.

To the professor who focuses on subject matter, neither the needs of the teacher nor those of the learner are permitted to reshape the material except in quite minor ways. Teachers who are subject-matter-oriented usually view with alarm any suggestion that the content of a course ought to be changed in order to facilitate the learning process. Changing subject matter to accommodate the special needs of students appears to them to be tampering with academic standards and, in the long run, to be detrimental to the students themselves. The teacher for whom this subject-matter or "principles and facts" prototype serves as a model is probably most typical among university professors. He is concerned with the systematic coverage of his subject, and he believes the primary function of the university teacher is to inform the student about this subject and provoke him into additional inquiry and discovery about it.

But those professors who emphasize one of the other components in the teaching-learning process contend that this principles-and-facts prototype is based largely on an academic myth. What, they ask, is "subject matter" anyway? They hold that the conventional perimeters and content of each field of knowledge are determined by historical accident and preserved with only minor revision and updating by the learned societies. Not holding subject matter coverage sacrosanct, they emphasize other elements of the teaching-learning process.

The teacher who focuses on the second element—the professor himself—believes that students and subject matter should accommodate themselves to him. He is, after all, the possessor of knowledge and insight, and a model for learners. To submit to alteration for the sake of the other two elements would be to surrender his ego. When, for example, a nationally famous American professor of French was reprimanded by his department chairman for not teaching his sophomore French class at an appropriately elementary level, he replied, "When a restaurateur hires an Escoffier, he does not expect him to make ordinary hamburgers!"

Such an instructor-centered teacher argues that if the professor is to be pushed into a shape that is not his own, his humanity and individuality will be lost and we might as well invest instead in more efficient types of programmed learning. He functions as a model inquirer. Not nearly as concerned as his principles-and-facts colleague with the systematic coverage of subject matter, he is satisfied to use samples of subject matter in demonstrating for his students the way an expert—namely, himself—deals with the problems presented by this material. Students and subject matter remain important for him, but *they* must be adjusted to fit what *he* is.

The third teaching prototype emphasizes the student. Student-centered professors argue that the teaching-learning process will not be effective if conditions require the student element to be vastly reshaped before the process can get started. Their view is that if the student is expected to accommodate himself to the other two elements in the educational transaction, if he is pushed into a shape other than his own, the whole educational process is endangered. The student's requirements—the steps needed for his development— are what is important. In this view, the whole undergraduate enterprise—classes and courses and professors—exists to meet the student's needs as a growing human being.

It became apparent during our investigation and analysis of student-centered teachers that a further classification was necessary. One type of professor emphasizes student development but limits his efforts to improving the student's mind. Class sessions of such a teacher are typically organized around his desire to help students acquire a set of intellectual skills and abilities. Students are taught to adopt reason and language as their primary tools and to use problem-solving as the major means of investigating subject matter. The second type of student-centered professor wants to help students develop as individuals, along all the dimensions—particularly the nonintellectual dimensions—where growth appears necessary or desirable. The student's peer group (his classmates in a given course, for example) is used as one of the means for accomplishing such development.

These teachers emphasize not *what* a student must know— subject matter—but *how* he is to acquire that knowledge. Those who emphasize the student-as-mind prototype encourage students to develop ease in a variety of intellectual skills—verbal, analytic, rational, scientific—and to move freely from formulating problems to analyzing data and testing solutions. In contrast, teachers who represent the student-as-person prototype treat the student not only as a "mind" but as an individual whose intellectual, emotional, aesthetic, and other developments are inseparable.

To summarize: among evocative teaching styles—the ones in which it is possible to rise to the level of art—there are four distinct prototypes. The most common is the principles-and-facts instructor. He has mastered the cognitive knowledge in his field, and he teaches what he knows. The second model—the instructor-centered prototype—also emphasizes cognitive knowledge, but his unique point of view and forceful personality organize the material in a special way. He teaches what he is. Of the two student-oriented models, the first focuses on the development of intellectual skills. He trains minds. The other student-oriented prototype is concerned with affective as well as cognitive knowledge. He works with students as people.

None of these four sets of teaching styles is intrinsically

superior to any of the others. Within each of the four modes of evocative teaching, the professor can perform well or poorly in motivating student learning through inquiry and discovery. Each mode has its peculiar excellence, and within each the professor can rise to the level of art.

evaluating teaching

During our investigation of teaching styles, we discovered a principle that subsequently became a central guideline in our entire study: when visitors observe a teacher in action, they find it impossible to understand why he is doing what he does, or to judge how well he is doing it, unless they have some idea of the prototype that serves as his model. This principle is so fundamental that no description or evaluation of any professor's teaching can disregard it.

A classroom observer can be thoroughly mystified by the behavior of a teacher whose poor control of technique or unfavorable external conditions prevent him from realizing, even to a minimal degree, his own image of the ideal teacher. What the professor actually does in the classroom, in such a case, gives completely unreliable clues to what he hoped to do; and these can lead the observer to an unsound analysis of the class session, a mistaken judgment about teaching quality—particularly the potential quality of this teacher—and poor advice as to the best means of improvement. All judgments about art are, of course, subject to this same kind of error, whether we are dealing with an improvisational art like teaching or with one of the conventional arts like painting. If a painter paints a dog which an art critic does not recognize as a dog but guesses is a rabbit, the critic performs a poor job of criticism by attacking the painter for having painted a misshapen rabbit. Since the critic has misunderstood the painter's intention, he is not in a position to give an accurate description of the work or a sound artistic judgment. So it is that the evaluator cannot understand what the professor is doing or judge his success in the classroom unless he has a fairly accurate picture of the teaching prototype the professor has in his mind.

We also learned from our interviews with faculty members that while the teaching prototype a particular professor follows may be fairly constant during a single period of his life, it can vary greatly from one period to another in his professional development.

In fact, if a faculty member is "exhibiting growth," as some faculty evaluation forms put it, then his vision of the ideal teacher, in all probability, will vary from one stage of his professional life to the next.

When a department chairman or a promotions committee evaluates a professor's teaching performance, such developmental possibilities are not always taken into consideration. Judgment about a professor's teaching ability cannot be made solely in terms of the image he holds of the ideal university teacher and how closely he succeeds in realizing that ideal. It must also take note of which way he is going in his development as teacher-artist and how fast he is moving. The judgment required of the evaluator in such circumstances is very much like that required of an automobile driver who is trying to avoid collision with another vehicle—he must know the direction and speed of the other vehicle as well as its precise location on the road. Judgments which take these factors into account may be devilishly difficult to make, yet their inclusion is essential if department chairmen and promotion and tenure committees are to arrive at wise judgments. They must look first at the professor's image of the ideal university teacher—enlisting his aid in reconstructing it if necessary—and then determine the degree to which external reality corresponds to that mental image, how it may be changing and developing, and how it affects his future and the future of his department and institution. Above all, department chairmen and promotions committees must ascertain how well the faculty member's own professional goals fit into the overall educational goals of the institution.

In the last analysis, it is the professor's own vision of himself at his best—the teacher prototype he has chosen to follow—that will most influence his development as a university teacher. And just as none of the four sets of teaching styles that we call "evocative" is superior to any other, so for certain purposes the expert teacher-craftsman and the lecturer-artist play indispensable roles in today's university. I predict their obsolescence in another generation or two, but for the immediate future they will continue to perform important instructional activities on every campus. Thus as we work to improve college and university teaching, it is crucial for decision-makers in higher education to keep before them the principle that there are different classroom styles and that each has its own excellence. Within the evocative teaching styles, each developing artist at teaching must build his unique mode—one that is right both for his institution and also for himself, the mode through which his own aesthetics of teaching is most completely realized.

Joseph Axelrod is professor of comparative literature and chairman of the department, California State University, San Francisco. He is also affiliated with the University of California, Berkeley, where he directed the research project on model building in undergraduate colleges of the Center for Research and Development in Higher Education. Readers will find a full-scale development of the ideas presented here in his book The University Teacher as Artist: Toward an Aesthetics of Teaching with Emphasis on the Humanities *(San Francisco: Jossey-Bass, 1973).*

Professors Brown, Epstein, and Johnson:
three faculty members who react to new student
interests in different ways, depending in part on their
own childhood, their attitude toward authority,
and their image of themselves as educators.

patterns of faculty response to growing student diversity

michael bloom
norbert ralph
mervin freedman

The faculty interviews we conducted in 1970-1972 as part of the Wright Institute study (described in the "Editor's Notes" and the first article) revealed that their institutions are more complex than they were a decade ago. Student needs are more diverse; institutional goals are less well defined; political pressures are more direct; and the role of faculty members is more amorphous. These interviews also indicated how greatly faculty members are influenced by the attitudes and behavior of their students. For example, when we asked them, "What advantages and satisfaction does your career offer you?" their answers centered on teaching and the human contact and interaction it offers. In response to the question, "What is the most important source of information to you in evaluating your teaching?" the majority of professors stressed face-to-face interaction with students.

Clearly, students are "significant others" for faculty; they have a powerful effect on the professional identity, self-esteem, and general sense of competence of their teachers. They can reinforce faculty outlooks or force reexamination of them. Like that of other individuals, a professor's sense of identity—his view of himself in the world—remains constant as long as there is continuity between the way significant others act toward him and how he expects them to act, based on past experience. But current students are making demands on professors that often are not consonant with faculty members' past experience. As a result, many professors gave evidence in our interviews that their old identities are being thrown into question.

When we analyzed their comments, three clear patterns of response to these changed student opinions emerged: (1) some faculty reject the new values of student culture and rigidly reaffirm their habitual ways of thinking and behaving; (2) others embrace the new values of student culture and reject their old professional identity; and (3) still others use the new student values as a stimulus for reevaluating their outlook and self-conception. They neither totally accept nor totally reject new views, but rather incorporate those that seem to have value for them without rejecting their previous sense of themselves.

patterns of adjustment

These three patterns have a great deal in common with Perry's (1970) conceptualization of how individuals adjust to novel experience—by assimilation and accommodation. To Perry, assimilation is a matter of selective inattention and attention: the individual tends to recognize in a new situation only those aspects that accord with his assumptions about the nature of social reality, thereby preserving the integrity and stability of these assumptions. This mode corresponds closely to that used by the first group of faculty members, who react to growing student diversity by reaffirming their existing outlooks. Individuals who adjust to novel situations in this assimilative way can maintain a sense of security by preserving the continuity of their assumptions, but only at the cost of ignoring the novelty of divergent experiences.

In contrast, the person who deals with novel experience by accommodation modifies his assumptions about the nature of social reality to incorporate the novel experience and reconstructs his model of reality to include it. The second group of faculty accommodate the greater diversity of students in this way, by totally realigning their identity to accord with them. This accommodative mode enables the person to enter new situations, experience their stimulation and challenge, and gain a sense of mastery over them; but if this mode is used exclusively, the individual loses the security and continuity of his old identity.

The third faculty pattern represents an adaptive equilibrium between assimilative and accommodative adjustment. Faculty members strive to maintain a sense of security and continuity while gaining mastery and expanded choice by confronting new student values. Needless to say, they do not acquire a condition of static adjustment, but rather dynamic equilibrium.

Before considering case examples of these three patterns of faculty response, several caveats require emphasis.

The authors of *The Authoritarian Personality* (Adorno and others, 1950) found that individuals have, in varying degrees, the disposition to assign positive values to groups with which they identify and negative ones to groups different from their own. Readers may experience an impulse to see the professors described in the following case histories as personifying positive or negative attributes. This is a natural tendency, but they should bear in mind that no one kind of faculty member is effective with all types of students.

Further, readers may view our types as static entities. In reality, they are functional behavior patterns; they exist in time and space and have evolved because they deal effectively with the environment. Each of the three patterns of faculty behavior described below can be seen as an adaptive response to the increasing diversification of students.

pattern one

The Case. The first pattern of faculty behavior is exemplified by Dr. Brown. She was an associate professor at the time of our interview, fifty years old, married with one child. She gives an immediate impression of having a great deal of commitment to and pride in her professional life. She states almost boastingly, "My husband feels I work too hard, but I love what I'm doing." Throughout the interview she stresses individuality and an active life. She grew up on a small ranch, and as a child she played outdoors much of the time, often alone. When her father worked around the yard, she would follow him everywhere. She identified closely with her father and states that she took after him in personality. Not particularly intellectual himself, he thought that education was a way to get ahead. She describes him as independent, industrious, and strong—qualities she tries to cultivate in herself—but she thinks he was too lenient in his dealings with her, although she was usually eager to please him.

Dr. Brown paints a very different picture of her mother and their relationship, which she describes as one of avoidance. She feels that her mother was too weak to deal with her. "My mother was dependent and gentle. I was a wild animal, hostile; I couldn't relate to her. She tried to be strict with me, to teach me manners, but she just couldn't."

In school Dr. Brown tried to do the best and be the best, receiving much encouragement and praise for her accomplishments, especially from her father. She remembers herself as always being a good student—"an achiever," as she puts it—and high grades were very important rewards for her. She most enjoyed school when she had difficult tasks to perform and could demonstrate her abilities in completing them. She found her graduate years were most pleasant for this reason. "I was a slave in grad school, but I loved it," she says.

Dr. Brown believes that the primary function of a college education is to develop professional competence in those students capable of strenuous intellectual work—"to achieve a high level of cold, professional, analytic functioning." She maintains that "in college one should be pushed to the edge of his intellectual capacity," and thus students who lack the capacity for high-level intellectual functioning or who do not intend to enter a career in which this capacity is necessary should not attend college. They overcrowd institutions, diluting their value for those who do have ability and intellectual goals. Dr. Brown says that grades are "not perfect," but are "valuable." They help motivate some students. Superior students, she believes, need to know they are superior, and grades are one way of telling them. "They need to be rewarded," she says.

She describes her relationship with students as one of mutual respect: "equal, but separate." She expects her students to refer to her as Doctor Brown, and she calls them Mr., Miss, or Mrs. As she puts it, "I respect them too much to call them by their first names."

Dr. Brown sees students today as "the same as always." She feels that most student activism is caused by "a few rabble-rousers and self-seeking faculty members." She states that she has not changed her teaching style in any way because of student pressure. To "encourage intellectual involvement" in her classes she lectures, takes her students on field trips, and provides them with resource material.

Dr. Brown has good relations with most colleagues in her department. She values faculty members who are dedicated to their work, their teaching, and their subject matter. She most admires those who are highly competent, who set high standards for themselves and their students. She is not concerned with their political and social views and believes that the classroom "should not be blurred" by a professor's views on these matters. She considers that her own political views are generally more conservative than those of most faculty members, although she regards herself as very liberal on some issues, such as civil rights and civil liberties.

Dr. Brown sees herself as being rather impersonal, unemotional, respectful, and respectable. Her evaluation of her own academic abilities is that she is "intelligent," although not "gifted," and most importantly a "hard worker." Regarding ways of improving herself, she would like to be more self-disciplined and organized in the things she does.

Student Views. Our studies of student response to different faculty members indicate that the kind of faculty member which Dr. Brown typifies appeals to students who come to college for information and skills—the same objectives that motivated her attendance. They share her goals of education and consequently view her as a good professor. For other students she may offer little. For them the pressing demand is finding out who they are, what they have to offer the world, and what the world has to offer them. They have come to college to find, in Erikson's terms, their "psycho-social identity." These students want to know how a subject relates to the world and to themselves before they are willing to study it. Its relevance is important to them. But because Dr.

Brown's type of professor knows implicitly what students should learn, this apparent aloofness is often a sore point with certain students and can lead to rebellion or alienation among them, as the following example illustrates:

Interviewer: What do you find to be the major problem or difficulty in your education?
Student: Professors who are rigid and traditional.
Interviewer: What do you mean by traditional?
Student: They are interested in relating facts rather than philosophies.
Interviewer: Why is this a problem?
Student: It stifles new ideas . . . it doesn't provide for individual needs. They are too impersonal. They don't care about the student as a person.

Some students unwillingly comply with the demands of these faculty members. Others avoid them. Still others who need to rebel against authority seek them out, finding a symbol of authority against which to exercise their feelings. Rebellion can take the form of classroom arguments over the relevance of the material or other disruptive outbursts. In some cases, confrontations between two viewpoints stimulate thought; in other cases, they restrict communication.

The Pattern. Faculty members characterized by this attitude commonly believe that what is most important in a college education is the acquisition of disciplinary knowledge and techniques for evaluating knowledge and that the student who gains such knowledge is well educated to function effectively in society. These professors consider themselves to be experts in a special field. They stress their responsibility for seeing that students get the knowledge and experience necessary for them to become expert as well. They feel that conventional grades are an appropriate measure of learning. Underlying this view of grades is a more general belief that there is a unitary set of goals within a discipline and absolute standards for evaluating them.

This first group of faculty members differs from those professors who believe that judgment is relative and therefore that one viewpoint may be "right" for them but not right for someone else. They are characterized by adherence to a fixed point of reference.

In our study we found that professors who share this view also tend to share similarities in background that may account at least partially for this position.

In Dr. Brown's past we see that she held her father in the greatest esteem. He had high expectations for her and praised her for performing well in her assigned tasks in school. The other important people in her formative years, her mother and her teachers, had similar expectations. She had no reason, therefore, to question their values. Furthermore, questioning these values would threaten the security she derived from her relationships with them. Even when she had become independent of her parents she found it difficult to question their values. To do so would perhaps entail rejecting many of the standards by which she evaluated herself. To say that conventional grades mean little can be very threatening for someone like Dr. Brown. She has based her sense of self-esteem on the assumption that the A grades she received for her work as a student means that she is a superior person—an authority.

It is easy to see why Dr. Brown claims that students today are no different from what they have always been—that is, that only a few "rabble-rousers" make students act differently. Students who are unconventional or difficult in one way or another are regarded as "sick" psychologically. Such a professor denies the validity of a student outlook that differs from his own. In Perry's terms, the professor assimilates these experiences within his present frame of reference—an effective way to eliminate situations that produce anxiety.

pattern two

The Case. Professor Epstein, just turned thirty when we interviewed her, teaches sociology in an interdisciplinary program. She was the only child of a Jewish family in a large Eastern city. In describing herself as a child she says: "I was a very good child, and virtually raised myself. I also was as stubborn as my old man. I was very alone." These early themes of being a good child and being lonely were important. The picture that emerges is of a child who internalized parental standards of good conduct very early and very thoroughly, in order to win affection from her parents, but who expressed hostility and aggression through stubbornness, as her father did. She coped with her sense of isolation and her desire to

be a good child in ways that validated her family's ethnic identity—
by intellectual activities. As she says, "I found myself in the situation of either going blind reading or being alone." She notes that
she loved school and read everything, and through these pursuits
she gained security and self-esteem. But her school experiences were
not untroubled or free of turmoil and ambivalent feelings. Stressful
events such as tests and the first days of the school year were
traumatic for her, causing her considerable distress.

The first three years of her graduate training at a large state
university were uneventful, but in the final years a major event
occurred: she became involved in the political unrest on her campus. Her participation in this struggle began a period of profound
change in her life, both personal and intellectual. She remembers
the camaraderie of the events, the joy of commonality of purpose
and outlook, without mentioning substantive events and issues. She
recalls gaining self-esteem and sense of purpose while associating
with like-minded friends, and remembers feeling: "I must be doing
something right. Look who my friends are. Incredible people!"

Intellectually she was greatly influenced by radical writers,
especially those of a Marxist persuasion. She mentions the writings
of Marcuse and Lenin as having a profound influence on her development. Radical action, radical peer-group affiliation, and radical
intellectual orientation all became part of a new identity. Her whole
value system was realigned in the way Erikson (1969) and Lifton
(1961) have so well described. In a period of political and social
controversy her total realignment served an adjustive purpose by
giving her a way of ordering experience and action. It provided
social support and an ideological system.

This restructuring of values can be understood in the context
of her past experiences. It was a way of achieving community and
companionship with peers, thereby overcoming years of loneliness.
A somewhat unsocial and bookish girl before her conversion to
radicalism, in the campus demonstrations an active, even flamboy-
ant character emerged. She describes this period as the most important of her life. Needless to say, it had a profound impact on her
teaching career.

Like most faculty members, as our research and that of
Gustad (1960) indicate, Miss Epstein did not make a conscious
decision to go into teaching. Rather, she drifted into it, first as a
part-time way to earn money, then as a full-time occupation. When

we asked her to describe her philosophy of education she replied: "Education is taking place in the streets; education means less and less what's going on in schools. The most important question is who you are and how do you want to get where you're going. The rest is foolishness or useless."

These remarks reflect her new ideological view of life and education. She completely rejects traditional forms of education. Her politically radical view of education is applied in other areas. She sees teaching as one way of organizing people for "the movement," and she would consider her courses and educational program a success if they "were a hotbed of political activity."

A feature of her new ideological perspective is a nondirective, even antiauthoritarian view of education. In answer to the question "How do you respond to the notion that students need structures and figures of authority in their lives?" she says: "Like a hole in the head. They don't need the type of authority that says you do this because I say so, or else. They need people to say this is the way I see things; this is the way I think things should be done. They need something they can identify with. The danger is that they will become wishy-washy." When asked how her philosophy of education expresses itself in the way she teaches, she answers, "I'm essentially nondirective. I ask kids what they want."

She describes with enthusiasm her methods for dealing with students. "They come to see me, the campus radical, and tell me they are upset, and I get them even more upset. I tell them the basic assumptions about American politics that we all know are wrong. They don't understand all the events on campuses that are happening around the nation. Some of them mean terribly well, and they think that teaching in the ghettoes is the answer; but they have to change their whole vision of the future, when they find out that this won't work and why." This ideological assault on views of conventional students is complemented by a personal style that is abrasive at times, as she herself realizes. Self-critically, she says, "If I wasn't so intimidating maybe I could get to more kids. . . . I tried to keep quiet this year but I was a failure," revealing the difficulty she encounters in trying to reconcile noncoerciveness with ideological fixity.

Student Views. Student reactions to Miss Epstein are extreme. She herself notes, "I'm rated A or F by students; there's no in-between." Many students in search of elements of a new identity are attracted to her because she seems to provide a philosophy of life that offers more than the traditional ideologies. These students feel they share common interests and concerns with her, and these feelings are reciprocated. But for a variety of reasons this initial enthusiasm declines markedly for some students. They seem to find her solutions too extreme—even occasionally frightening—and in various ways, ranging from apathy to antagonism, dissociate themselves from the impact of her teaching. They conclude that answers have to be found elsewhere. Searching for a post-conventional identity, they may wish to find a teacher who not only affirms the value of the journey but gives them some sense of a final destination. Her contact with more conventional students is slight. These students are enrolled in other schools or departments of the university and rarely select her classes. Wishing to implement conventional roles in conventional ways, they are not interested in her attempts to develop new definitions of life and education.

The Pattern. Faculty members such as Professor Epstein—the accommodators—deal with new and radical definitions of education and life by embracing these changes and substantially modifying their professional identities. They often characterize themselves as good children who internalized clearly defined parental standards of right and wrong rather early in life, but who did so ambivalently. They acquiesced to parental sanctions but with an inner sense of rage and rebellion. They were dutiful students whose success in school was admired by parents, and this dutiful orientation to education served to carry them through graduate school. During their early professional training they developed a conventional professional identity. But their identification with professional standards, like their feelings about parents, was not without ambivalence. They experienced tension between professional role definitions and their own sense of integrity. This ambivalence was not resolved, and they continued to endure a sense of alienation from the dominant outlook of their profession.

The rise of radical perspectives on education and society has aroused considerable personal conflict in these faculty members. Radical alternatives make possible a new commitment, one with more intrinsic meaning and one that appears to offer at least a partial solution to the tension between self and society. An individual who commits himself totally to radical ideology may thereby circumvent tension and ambivalence. A faculty member who adopts these alternatives adjusts to the complexities of campus life by rigidly accommodating his frame of reference to radical perspectives. Any vestiges of traditional categories of thought and action are intolerable, and he becomes radical with a vengeance.

The evolution of this new self-definition of Dr. Epstein and faculty members like her results from self-questioning and face-to-face interaction with students in the classroom. Since the personality development of these faculty members is close to that of students, the same types of conflict concern them both: dissatisfaction with traditional models of education as well as with conventional identities. They are searching for a new commitment in a new frame of reference. When confronted with students offering radical alternatives, these faculty members, who have viewed education in traditional terms for most of their professional life, find that these new definitions provide a framework for thought and action and a partial solution for their own developmental problems. Instead of restricting interaction with students to avoid the threat of redefinition, as professors in Pattern One tend to do, faculty members such as Dr. Epstein find mutual affirmation of emergent identities in their relations with students. Their reference group is no longer their profession and colleagues but students in search of postconventional identities.

pattern three

The Case. Dr. Johnson has been teaching for fifteen years, usually in traditional educational settings. During the past few years, however, he has been a faculty member of an innovative undergraduate college devoid of standard curriculum and grades. Faculty members exhibiting this third pattern of response are by no means all located in "alternative" educational institutions. Some are engaged in traditional educational activities in conventional settings. But Dr. Johnson came to this college in search of new ways to do things. He is not convinced that its program will work out to his satisfaction, but sees it as a challenge that could bring the educational process closer to his ideals.

Johnson was a serious child—too serious, he says. He thinks that he grew up too fast, being ambitious from an early age, although he got along fairly well with his peers.

The usual role models in his household were reversed, Johnson states. His mother tended to be dominant and his father submissive. As a result he lacked respect for his father, although they were close and his father was always warm and supportive, no matter what he did. Dr. Johnson recalls his father as intellectual and industrious and his mother, on the other hand, as driving, shrewd, and more socially conforming than his father. He respected her for these qualities, and today he believes he is overtly most like his mother in energy and drive—although in less obvious ways, he has much of his father's character.

Dr. Johnson was always encouraged by his parents to do well in school. They considered it to be his best avenue for upward social mobility, and he accepted this belief without question. His consistently high achievement was taken for granted. Now he thinks that he would have been better off had he rebelled. He believes he got good grades because he knew how to "play the game well," not because of intrinsic interest in his studies. In college the professor who had most educational impact on him was a male speech teacher who drew out his individuality and encouraged him to develop a distinctive style of speech that is effective in communication.

With respect to professional commitment, Johnson states, "I wanted to become a teacher out of a desire to work with people who are growing and for whom academic work would be a projection of their own interests and concerns." He is most interested in students who come to college to find a relationship between their "inner direction and the academic and artistic world." He feels that enhancing the ability to be economically productive is, of course, valuable, but he believes colleges presently provide ample opportunity for professionalization. He had earned a Ph.D. in sociology and worked for many years as a faculty member before he gave much critical thought to the value of colleges and universities for himself and the world at large. He joined the faculty of the innovative college because of the "failure of conventional educational institutions to deal with the growing need of students to evaluate things before accepting them."

In recent years he has increasingly questioned the way he was treated in school—that is, as an "urn to be filled with the rich juices of knowledge." He found this process comfortable both as a student and as a teacher, but now he finds it unsatisfying. In his first years as a faculty member he met many students who, in his opinion, were in college primarily to obtain a "union card" for a better

job and not for the intrinsic value of study. He taught in a traditional manner—presenting materials and giving grades—and although
he felt that something was missing, at the time he did not have the
social and intellectual context or the personal understanding to
change.

Many students in Johnson's present school come to pursue
personal development, either exclusively or in addition to vocational goals. With these students, he sees his role as being less defined
than it used to be. He has held classes that presented theoretical
matter intertwined with personal experiences. He has taught outside
his academic discipline on various occasions. One group of students
put on a television play, another took up his long-standing interest
in jazz after learning that he had worked his way through college
playing the saxophone.

Johnson now sees himself primarily as an "educator," a facili-
tator of the growth of his students' potential, rather than a member
of a professional discipline. His move away from the traditional role
of professor resulted from years of reevaluation of past activities
and values but was partly stimulated by his placing himself in situations that were different from any he had previously experienced—
for example, encounter groups and experimental classes. These experiences were often very uncomfortable for him, but the insights
he gained made them worthwhile. As a result, Johnson has concluded that the really important aspect of the educational process is
the teacher's ability to be "open" with students. He believes he
should show them both why he is interested in things and how he
goes about mastering them. Johnson finds that being open is not
always easy. He states that he, like everyone else, has some areas of
insecurity. In engaging in free exchanges on both subject matter and
personal values, he finds that these insecurities may become pain-
fully exposed, but not without benefit, since this exposure has
sparked his own personal development as well as that of his students.

Since he views the value of various educational experiences as
somewhat relativistic and personal, Dr. Johnson considers grades to
have little meaning. He believes, however, that students desire and
need evaluation and criticism. He holds that a teacher must first
gain a student's respect by allowing the student to see that his
opinions have value, and only then proceed to challenge his ideas.
In an intellectual encounter based on respect the weakness of an

argument becomes evident, and the student is motivated to improve his understanding of a topic. In Johnson's opinion, the evaluation implicit in challenging discussion has more meaning than grades because students are reevaluating and criticizing the ideas with which they are most concerned. He thinks students are basically curious and therefore eager to test their ideas, and he has found that if they are given a chance to do so, they will hound a professor for criticism.

Johnson believes that many more students today, in comparison with those he taught fifteen years ago, are going to college to gain some awareness of themselves and their world. He finds that current students have greater self-direction, and he feels stimulated by them. He believes that his teaching style has much to offer them and that they, in turn, have much to offer him. He thinks student activism on campus results from frustration with colleges that do not look on students as individuals.

Student Views. Students' reactions to this type of professor, like their response to our two previous groups of faculty, are diverse. For students who come to college to gain information and skills, the interest of these professors in relating intellectual endeavor to personal life may seem to be a waste of time or even a threat. These students may view the relativism expressed by these teachers as evidence of incompetence. Often they prefer to see intellectual material presented in less ambiguous ways. As a result, students who see college primarily as preparation for a job are likely to avoid this third group of professors, if they can.

Radical students, as well, are likely to criticize these faculty members. They are searching for definitive grounds on which to base their condemnation of society. The relativistic and complex views of these professors seem weak to them. Also, they may consider the disposition of these teachers to see things in terms of personal responsibility as antagonistic to their desire to regard things as entirely socially determined.

For students who view college as a chance for further personal development, this type of professor is often held in high esteem, as the following passage indicates:

Interviewer: Can you describe the best teacher you've had here?

Student: He knows his area; he knows how to learn

from the student; how to draw the student out. He's warm and inviting. He's curious. He's concerned for the student.

These students themselves often are reevaluating their past. They see that some professors can understand their questioning and their problems. If they allow themselves to become familiar with such a faculty member (which is usually easier than with teachers who are more defensive), they may recognize that he has gained some satisfaction from his way of thinking and looking at the world. He does not demand acceptance of his outlook; rather he offers it to them for their inspection. They may find that he has dealt with the same problems they are facing and that he has discovered some satisfactory resolutions.

The Pattern. Faculty members such as Dr. Johnson, in accord with their belief that personality development—the integration of personal needs and intellectual endeavor—is the major educational task among many students today, see education as the joint responsibility of student and teacher. These professors believe that students have some awareness of their own educational needs and that, with the aid of their teachers, they can develop procedures for satisfying them. They hold that these educational procedures can be developmental for the teacher as well.

Faculty members who exemplify this pattern of behavior do not abandon discussion of facts and theory, but integrate such discussions with accompanying feelings. Dr. Johnson, for instance, explicates and discusses sociological theory. He believes, however, that such presentation is of little value unless he tells something about how sociological theory has influenced his world view and his identity within it. Such professors see themselves offering for the scrutiny of others the theories and views that have been useful, exciting, and productive for them. They tend to see student rebellion as an opportunity for testing ideas and values. They are usually open to students' views, but they are not necessarily persuaded by them. They appear to be able to cope with challenge to their own ideas, because their self-esteem seems to be based, at least in part, on confidence in their ability to adjust to novel situations rather than on their expertise alone.

These professors have high expectations for themselves. Since their past goals have been altered as a result of their reevaluation, however, they are skeptical of holding goals as absolute. Therefore, their views of education are characterized by some relativism.

One characteristic in their past that may make it possible for them to be self-critical is their parental relationships. Whereas parents of faculty in the first group gave their love and esteem in exchange for accomplishment, the professors in this group felt that at least one of their parents would give them love and esteem no matter what they did. For example, although Dr. Johnson did not respect his father because he was too easygoing, he was completely secure in his father's love for him. Like many of these professors, Johnson seems to have internalized high expectations from his mother but a sense of freedom from his father. The parental roles of the mothers and fathers of similar professors may not be similarly reversed, but they are commonly differentiated, producing internalized tension between high expectation and warm acceptance on almost any terms.

This combination of high personal ideals and the confidence to examine past experiences and experiment with new ones is central to the personalities of faculty members like Johnson. The skeptical milieu of present academic culture appears to have provided the opportunity for many to begin this pattern of reevaluation and experimentation. Inasmuch as this experience has been valuable for them, they wish to provide the same opportunity for their students.

developmental transition

We became aware in examining our case histories that what we originally saw as three separate patterns were in fact interrelated if we viewed them from a developmental perspective. Each pattern may be conceptualized as occupying a different position along a theoretical continuum. The primary issue of this transition is the tension between self and society—that is between the opportunities and limitations that contemporary social roles offer and the individual's sense of identity and integrity (Keniston, 1970). Not everyone addresses this conflict, but if an individual does confront the developmental issues of this stage, he is working out his own unique style of commitment to the existing roles and institutions of his culture.

In a recent interview with Robert Coles Father Daniel Berrigan posed the essentials of the developmental issues that professors, and, indeed, all professionals, must face in their training:

Professional education in America, maybe everywhere, is both valuable and dangerous because one acquires important tools, but one has to fight hard to stay loyal to one's values, to stay spiritually alive. That training at least gives one the ability to *do* something, and also gives one a certain world view, a certain limited but important competence; but that training must now itself be submitted to scrutiny and evaluation and examination [Berrigan and Coles, 1971].

Here Berrigan, a man who has obviously confronted these issues in the most profoundly personal way, is describing a tension between the demands of society and one's sense of self. As Berrigan states, professional training endows an individual with competence, but it may also give him a world view that submerges his own values and integrity. If it does, the professional makes decisions among options in accord with professional priorities, rather than with personally and self-consciously determined priorities. As Heiss (1970) documents in her survey of graduate education, the socializing forces of graduate training are powerful, and can be dehumanizing and limiting when advancement of the profession is championed as the paramount goal.

In describing this developmental transition we can distinguish between a conventional and a post-conventional level of professional development.* At the conventional stage of development there is no tension between the individual's definition of self and those definitions offered by his professional reference group. These reference group definitions are seen as absolutes, as givens which are essentially unquestionable. An individual at a post-conventional stage of professional development has dealt with this tension and found ways of resolving it. As Keniston points out, this individual may become a dedicated revolutionary or dedicated to the conventional social order, but he does so out of a sense of free choice. Since he is not motivated out of a fear of the self becoming submerged by the authority of social conventions, he need not rebel. Neither does he conform out of fear of losing the esteem of authorities. Because this individual has questioned professional definitions and realizes that these roles and conventions are but a subset of all possible identities, he or she can evolve the style of adaptation which represents a personal ordering of priorities.

*The terms *conventional* and *post-conventional* are Kohlberg's and Gilligan's (1971).

Dr. Brown, our prototypic professor of Pattern One, is at a conventional stage of professional development. As Perry (1970) points out, individuals at this stage have an essentially dualistic world view; for her the world is divided into good and bad by some authority—in this case the standards of her professional reference group. Because she has never questioned her own values, she cannot really imagine that other kinds of values might have some validity. She dismisses the new diversity of student culture by saying "students are the same always," and only "a few rabble-rousers and self-seeking faculty members" cause the troubles on campuses. In relying on the assimilative mode exclusively she can deny that anything has "really" changed, and she can maintain the security of her old views. Her unwillingness to question professional standards originates, at least in part, in her unquestioning acceptance of the values and standards of parents and school authorities.

Pattern Two, of which Professor Epstein is the chief protagonist, represents a transitional stage between conventional and postconventional professional development. In her early graduate career the values to which she adhered were largely conventional. But her identification with professional standards, like her earlier identification with the standards of parents and school authorities, was ambivalent. While she acquiesced to them outwardly, inwardly she experienced at times a sense of rage and a disposition to reject these standards. Confrontation with radical values, as presented to her by peers, was intense and upset her usual modes of adjustment. Since assimilation was impossible, some form of accommodation was necessary. But her internal ambivalence would not allow for partial or synthetic solutions. She could attain independence from conventional standards and deal with internal ambivalence only by a totalistic accommodation to these new ideologies of life and education. Her views of the world had changed greatly, but it is difficult to say whether any real developmental gains were made. Her outlook was still dualistic and therefore *structurally* similar to Dr. Brown's, although in content it was diametrically opposed. She saw conventional academic standards and a traditional world view as totally wrong, and the new values and ideologies of her peer or reference group as totally right.

The faculty member exemplifying our third and last pattern, Dr. Johnson, has evolved a personal style of adaptation to his role as a professor one with which he can sustain his sense of integrity in relation to professional goals. He is at a post-conventional stage of professional development. He is able to question his own professional commitments and their relevance to larger social questions, and he does not hold his own values as absolute. This pattern represents a sympathetic rather than a rigid or arbitrary response to the new values and diversity of student culture. While he can accommodate the changes he considers valuable, he continues to affirm traditional values of academic achievement and standards from which he has gained self-esteem in the past. This freedom of judgment and the opportunity to exercise autonomy in meeting standards have their origins in Dr. Johnson's childhood and youth.

conclusion

In this paper we have examined the relation of personality change to changing social reality in a sample of college professors. We believe that the faculty members we have described exemplify certain difficulties or confusions that all professors undergo in some form. We should like to emphasize that faculty members who may be classified in each pattern have qualities that are valued by some students. No one pattern is effective with all students, and each has its function in today's university. In presenting these patterns we hope that professors may come to understand how certain social changes affect their personal lives and professional careers.

references

Adorno, T. W., Frenkel-Brunswik, E., Levinson, D., and Sanford, N. *The Authoritarian Personality.* New York: Harper, 1950.

Berrigan, D., and Coles, R. "Dialogue Underground: II." *New York Review of Books,* 1971, *16*(5).

Erikson, E. *Identity: Youth and Crisis.* New York: Norton, 1969.

Gustad, J. W. *Career Decisions of College Teachers.* SREB Research Monograph Series No. 2, Atlanta: Southern Regional Education Board, 1960.

Heiss, A. *Challenges to Graduate Schools.* San Francisco: Jossey-Bass, 1970.

Keniston, K. "Youth As a Stage of Life." *The American Scholar,* 1970, *39*(4).

Kohlberg, L., and Gilligan, C. "The Adolescent As Philosopher: The Description of Self in a Post-Conventional World." *Daedalus,* 1971, *100*(4), 1015-1086.

Lifton, R. *Thought Reform and the Psychology of Totalism.* New York: Norton, 1961.
Perry, W. *Forms of Intellectual and Ethical Development During the College Years.* New York: Holt, Rinehart, and Winston, 1970.

Michael Bloom is a graduate student and research assistant at the Wright Institute in Berkeley. A Ph.D. candidate thinking of teaching and clinical practice, he is broadly interested in developmental psychology throughout life. Norbert Ralph, also a Ph.D. candidate at the Wright Institute, has worked for the past three years studying college faculty and experimental education. He plans to train counselling psychology students to work in higher education as experts in human development.

A professor's understanding of his own childhood and education can make him a more effective teacher, and planners must take these early experiences into account if institutional changes are to mesh with long-standing faculty needs.

personal history and professional career

michael bloom
mervin freedman

Our interest in studying the personal histories of professors has grown out of our observation that what professors try to provide for their students is primarily what college gave them—or, in some cases, what they feel was missing during their college years. How the past relates to the present varies with individuals; what remains consistent, however, is this relationship between the college experience and present educational stance.

In examining the actions of individuals or groups, some scholars tend to negate the importance of the past, believing that what people do or will do is freely chosen. Contrarily, others exaggerate the influence of the past, claiming, for example, that people have no control over their behavior (and therefore no responsibility for it), since it was predetermined by their upbringing. We find that the past is not all-determining. Faculty members obviously can change and develop; but we observe that their choice of an academic career, as opposed to some other vocation, and their teaching style have roots in their developmental histories. Their past, therefore, strongly affects their attitudes toward education, and their own educational background is likely to provide the foundation for their relationship with students.

By understanding the influences of the past, faculty members can comprehend their present needs more completely, and such increased understanding can lead to greater effectiveness in meeting them. Moreover, this insight is likely to heighten their awareness of students' needs and the best ways to satisfy them as well.

In this article, we describe some developmental experiences and characteristics that faculty seem to have in common and then turn to some features that seem to distinguish subgroups of professors. We start out with parental relations, since these are the first important ones in a child's life and, in some respects, the prototype of all others.

Almost all the faculty members we interviewed as part of the Wright Institute study (described in the first article) felt that they had had good relations with at least one and usually with both of their parents. As they recall the situation, fathers were more aloof than mothers, and the relationship with the mother was considered closer than that with the father. Fatherly aloofness, however, was not symptomatic of a bad relationship, faculty report: their fathers displayed good will toward them, despite their reserve. Even faculty members who are critical of some aspects of their upbringing generally experienced good will from their parents.

Almost all the parents valued intellectual pursuits, school achievement, or both. (We distinguish between intellectual pursuits and school achievement because some faculty members recall identifying with their parents' interest in books and intellectual activity generally, although their parents never directly encouraged them to do well in school.) Certainly parental values are likely to have considerable impact if a child esteems the parent, and since most faculty members thought well of their parents, they were disposed to emulate them in valuing intellectual and academic achievement.

During their primary and secondary school years some faculty members experienced rebellious feelings toward school, and a number wished they had openly rebelled. However, nearly all of them were highly motivated to do well academically before they had ever contemplated an academic career; furthermore, nearly all received some esteem in school for doing well. Some had to work hard for this recognition, while for others recognition came easily. Recognition further encouraged them to continue academic pursuits.

Something else shared by nearly all professors is the presence of a particularly important faculty member in their lives. When asked whether any teacher had had a significant effect on them during undergraduate or graduate school, almost every professor said yes. They report being influenced by such qualities as integrity, intellectual commitment, and clarity of thought. They admired those characteristics they saw as important or essential to their own development. For many faculty members the importance of this identification persists to this day in their attempt to be for their students what this influential professor was to them.

Faculty members share a belief that a primary tool for improving the world is a better understanding of it and that such knowledge is most valuable when shared by a large number of people. When asked what they see as the value of a college education, most of them emphasize the value of knowledge either for the individual or for society at large.

coping with the world

We propose that this belief system is rooted in the developmental history of the professor. Many things frighten a child as he develops. In his earliest years he looks to his parent or parental surrogates for protection. However, as he grows older, he wishes to deal with his fears more autonomously, and he must learn to do so. Many mechanisms can be used to control this fear, and all are functional to varying degrees in different circumstances. For example, the child can deny fearful feelings and continue his activity without allowing the anxiety to intrude into his consciousness. All of us have had the experience of being challenged to do something of which we were afraid, and of having to convince ourselves that we were not afraid before we could meet the challenge. Another way to handle fear is to try to gain control over it through action. Children who are afraid of water can master this fear by learning how to swim. Fear can also be dealt with through understanding. When we know how something works, its outcomes become predictable, and we can prepare for them. As children grow up they depend increasingly on those methods for controlling fear that seem to be most effective for them. We believe the development of faculty members has predisposed them to rely primarily on intellectual mastery in dealing with life's challenges.

For example, one professor of biology sees some of the origins of his interest in biology in an experience he had when he was fifteen. His father had a mild heart attack and was hospitalized. For several days the son was not allowed to visit his father and he felt panicked with fear. Not knowing what to do with himself, he went to the library and read everything he could find on heart attacks. He then called the doctor and asked him specific questions about his father's condition. Following this conversation he felt much better. His continuing dedication to the study of biology commenced at that time. If this professor had been allowed to participate in his father's care (thus dealing with anxiety through action), perhaps he would have become a physician instead.

Though most faculty members have not experienced comparably dramatic events demonstrating the power and utility of knowledge, their faith in its value seems to stem from rewards they received from intellectual activity in their childhood and adolescence. All in all, then, professors share a number of common experiences in their past which seem to have contributed to their development as faculty members.

subgroup differences

Contrarily, professors have some diverse educational outlooks and goals which also have developmental origins. The most obvious and widely studied of these differences occur, of course, among the academic disciplines: between scientists and humanists, for example, or between physicists and chemists (Roe and Siegelman, 1964; Bereiter and Freedman, 1962). Differences also separate research-oriented professors from teachers and "cosmopolitan" faculty from "local"-oriented faculty. We found, however, in our interviews, that differences also exist between the faculties of different *institutions*. We turn now to a discussion of three such groups of faculty: first those who are characteristic of medium-sized midwestern state universities; then those at small liberal arts colleges; and finally, professors at large and prestigious research universities.

Midwestern State University. The great majority of faculty members at Midwestern State University (MSU) grew up in the Midwest in homes not particularly different from those of the general population in that area. Most are from either lower-middle-class or middle-class families. Rural and urban settings are represented almost equally. They see their parents as "not intellectual." Family politics seem to reflect those of the Midwest in general, with most parents being on the moderate to conservative end of the political spectrum.

Faculty members on the whole say that their childhoods were happy and sociable. They frequently were involved in school and church activities, clubs, and sports. And most reported a happy home life within a close family. They had considerable respect for both parents. Discipline came from either parent, usually in the form of physical punishment or a verbal reprimand. Very few mention unjust treatment by parents; most feel they got what they deserved.

One professor described his parents this way: "I had a good deal of respect for my father. He had the strongest ethics of anyone I've ever known. I always looked up to him. . . . I was very close to my mother. She had a great deal of understanding. She never went to college but was determined that her children would have the opportunity." He went on to describe parental discipline: "If I ever did get punished I usually got spanked; I almost never did get punished though. I knew what was expected of me and I usually did it."

Although parents were not intellectuals themselves, most of them encouraged their children to do well in school and to go to college—but more out of a desire to see them advance in status and wealth rather than out of intrinsic interest in knowledge. With this backing most faculty members were good students throughout their school years. Most adhered to the belief that school was all right, and in any case they thought schools could not be changed.

Since they did not come from backgrounds of high social status, they were likely to be cautious in establishing relationships with teachers or professors. Yet by the time they finished high school, most had met a teacher who took a special interest in them, although others did not encounter such a teacher until college. Usually their mentor took the initiative by saying, essentially, "You've got what it takes to get where I am." Such encouragement was frequently what stimulated them to pursue further education in their chosen field.

In short, formal education has loomed very large in the lives of the MSU faculty: they derived much esteem from scholastic success, and college and graduate school carried them from a rather uneducated home with fairly low social prestige to a considerable degree of intellectual sophistication and status.

MSU professors report that college was more enjoyable than graduate school, and to a considerable degree this experience accounts for their presence at MSU, where undergraduate education is stressed. They wish to teach students from backgrounds similar to their own. They seem to wish to provide for students what college gave them—the opportunity to gain the education needed for upward mobility and a greater awareness of the world. They do not expect their students to come to college with an intrinsic desire for knowledge. They would like to create this interest in much the same way it was created for them, although they are well aware that some students will never develop such an interest. They feel it is valuable to provide these students with a certain amount of information and competence, and with a college degree. If nothing else, they believe college will help them better themselves socially and economically.

At times these faculty complain of student apathy, and they are eager to learn of ways to get students more involved in academic concerns. In general, however, they believe that college is a valuable experience for students, as it was for them, and they see little need for major changes on campus.

Private Liberal Arts College. The next group of professors is found in the private liberal arts college. Here, faculty are likely to come from middle-class and upper-middle-class homes and many geographical regions. Their parents were usually self-employed businessmen, educators, and professionals who had intellectual or artistic interests which they encouraged their children to cultivate and pursue for their own enjoyment rather than for social or economic advancement. Parents usually took for granted that their children would do well in school. The children did a considerable amount of reading, played musical instruments, and developed other intellectual and aesthetic interests aside from school.

These professors recall that they generally did well academically, although a large number sometimes felt indifferent to school or even rebellious. These periods did not reflect attenuated intellectual or aesthetic interest, but rather a reaction to a particular teacher or social setting. These faculty members report having felt somewhat different or apart from other students, particularly in high school. They had less interest in social functions and more interest in intellectual and aesthetic endeavors than most of their peers. As a result, they sensed themselves as social isolates, usually having a small group of close friends with like interests. Not until college did they find a comfortable social environment where they encountered a sizable number of students with whom they had much in common. Moreover, in college their intellectual and aesthetic interests were accorded considerable recognition.

The teacher or professor with whom they most readily identified was usually very competent and interested in intellectual matters as well as in his students. He was seen as being very involved and satisfied in his career, and he encouraged them to consider one like it. Encouragement from such an admired faculty member meant a great deal and conveyed to his students that the life of a professor was a good one.

For most of these faculty members, college was the place where and the time when they began to feel comfortable being identified as "intellectual." It is not surprising, therefore, that they wish to center their life in a college society. In addition to peers with whom they can share interests and a stimulating environment which rewards their competence and performance, the college culture provides other things they consider essential. When asked what advantages and satisfactions their career offered them, almost all mentioned autonomy and the freedom to pursue their own interests. As we indicated earlier, throughout their development their intellectual interests were rather independent of their school participation. Therefore, they enjoy having this autonomy and independence confirmed and supported.

These professors derive a great deal of satisfaction from teaching. Students provide them with intellectual stimulation plus an appreciative audience for their academic and aesthetic enthusiasm. The characteristic they "like best" in students is intellectual curiosity. They tend not to care for those who attend college primarily for vocational and social advancement. Students of this kind offer little stimulation, and these professors tender them little admiration in return; between them there is not much meeting of the minds. These faculty members like close intellectual relationships with like-minded students, while at the same time maintaining some personal distance from students. They say they have little or no desire to teach in institutions, such as research universities, which foster considerable academic competitiveness, as they believe competition depreciates the intrinsic joy of the intellect.

These professors, on the whole, tend to resist the pressures for change that are being felt on many campuses today. Because they value intellectual and scholarly achievement in and of itself, they are likely to oppose making their subject matter "relevant." Moreover, since their relationships with others have been based on shared intellectual interests, they often do not care to focus on personal encounters and feelings in relationships with students. They have chosen academic culture as the setting in which they want to live, and thus they are skeptical of forces that would alter the academic milieu they value so highly.

Large, Prestigious Research University. The family backgrounds of faculty members from these universities are in many ways similar to those of faculty at private liberal arts colleges: they tend to come from middle-class or upper-middle-class homes and from no specific areas of the country, and their fathers were self-employed businessmen, teachers, professionals, and corporate executives. One important difference between these two faculty subgroups, however, is that a significant number of fathers of university faculty worked for large corporations, whereas a corporate association was rare among fathers of our college faculty sample. Parents of the research-university professors are described as intellectuals less frequently than are parents of liberal arts college faculty, although they were more intellectually inclined than the MSU professors' parents.

In descriptions of their parental relations, one factor stands out very clearly: they feel their parents had high expectations of them. For some these expectations centered only on academic performance; for others they were more pervasive. Some parents demanded success openly; others simply conveyed that they were hurt when their children performed poorly. Although some children rebelled against these expectations, most of them did not wish to disappoint their parents. As they grew up their desire to do well became more and more internalized, and most of them now demand much of themselves. One professor laughingly remarks: "I've been a professor for ten years now; I've received a good deal of renown for my work from my colleagues; and still my parents recently asked me, why, if I was going to work so hard to become a doctor, didn't I become a *real* doctor?" Although this professor could laugh about his parents' question, he did so only after prefacing it with a statement delineating his actual successes.

The self-expectation of these professors has been not only to do well in a given area but to be among the best. Academia, however, was not necessarily a central focus for their ambitions in early school years. A wide variety of pursuits, many of them not particularly intellectual—such as athletics, school government, and scouts— occupied their attention. As a result, although the majority report having done well academically in high school, a significant number did not do well until college because their other activities were more interesting. For them, academic interest was a late development. But whatever the object of their attention, they pursued it with great vigor; in school the classes in which they did well were usually the ones they enjoyed the most. It is difficult to know whether their success in a class encouraged them to pursue the subject further, but the combination of success in a school subject, recognition for this success, plus personal interest in the particular subject seems to have encouraged them to pursue the subject through the Ph.D.

In college these faculty members were most influenced by professors who had achieved status in their field. They especially identified with professors who had high expectations for their students; they tried to meet or exceed their high academic standards. These professors may or may not have been good teachers, but they served as a model of what a successful professor should be.

Most of these faculty members considered their graduate years to be the most enjoyable of their educational experience. There they were able to concentrate on the academic areas that most stimulated them and in which they felt they could succeed. Moreover, graduate school provided the opportunity to associate most closely with the professors they admired. This affinity for their graduate days prompted them to seek jobs in universities where they could continue their intellectual pursuits among companions of intellectual and academic renown. In general, they became professors not out of a desire to teach but rather out of their interest in a discipline and their ambition to become successful scholars and researchers.

Faculty members at the research-oriented university indicate that they experience much stress in their professional lives and usually work many more than forty hours a week. Our interviews suggest that this stress results from their high goals for themselves. No matter what their accomplishment, it is not likely to measure up to their expectations.

Even though research takes precedence over teaching, for these professors, students do play a significant role in their lives because their self-concept of a good scholar includes the importance of making knowledge and insights available to others. They believe that the higher the level of competence they attain in a subject the more they can offer to students. The shared interest and respect they desire in return come primarily from students already committed to certain academic and intellectual interests. Such students, of course, are likely to be graduate students, and the major educational efforts of these faculty members are directed toward them. Like their own mentors in their own graduate years, they expect a lot of their graduate students, and they reward them for their achievements. They wish to provide the competence and encouragement required to help their students prepare for academic or comparable careers. In general, they express little desire for change on campus. In their view the universities have done and are doing a good job of education and research.

conclusion

The childhood and youth of faculty members predispose them to select an academic career—and certain kinds of academic institutions, at that. And as part of an academic culture they proceed to reinforce its norms and standards. Because the needs of faculty members are reasonably well met by this culture they tend to take a conservative stance rather than risk their satisfactions on uncertain innovations. When one is contemplating or proposing changes in a college or university it is well to keep these factors in mind. The scholarly life satisfies needs of faculty members of long standing—from as far back as infancy. A change can be developmental or threatening, depending on the individual's desire and capacity to adapt to it. If a faculty member's needs and the proposed changes are far apart, the changes will be perceived as a threat and resisted.

If one is to have a chance to alter academic culture, he must take into consideration these long-standing needs of faculty, as well as the desires of students. Too often plans have not borne fruit because reformers asked faculty members to relinquish important needs without providing ways to modify them or satisfy them by other means. Under such circumstances one may be sure that faculty members will find ways to meet their needs, often at the expense of planned change or reform.

We do not feel that all attempts at change are necessarily doomed to failure because of overpowering resistance. We have made these cautionary statements because too often faculty embark upon innovation with naive, utopian expectations (see the companion article on innovation in this issue) and college administrators often expect change to take place by decree. We, in fact, have talked to faculty who have greatly altered their educational outlook. These professors were willing participants in change, and their environments allowed them latitude to experiment and fail. They found that increased understanding of their needs greatly aided them in seeing alternative ways of meeting them, some far superior to their usual ways of doing things. Change does not come easily as a rule, but it does happen, often with considerable reward for the faculty member involved.

references

Bereiter, C., and Freedman, M. B. "Fields of Study and the People in Them." In N. Sanford (Ed.), *The American College.* New York: Wiley, 1962.
Roe, A., and Siegelman, M. *The Origins of Interests.* Washington, D. C.: American Personnel and Guidance Association, 1964.

*The professional development of the professor
cannot be equated with his self-assurance as
a teacher or his command of a discipline;
rather it is revealed in the complexity of his
personality and thought and his ability
to help students develop themselves.*

stages of
faculty development

norbert ralph

The subject of faculty development clearly is gaining prominence in the field of higher education, as this volume attests, but its meaning is not so clear. Very often the term mirrors commonsense ideas of mental health and adjustment and thus refers to ways in which faculty can learn to function more effectively with minimum stress and tension. While this definition is useful for many purposes, it does not adequately touch one essential facet of the development of faculty members (or human beings at large, for that matter): the growth of increasingly complex ways of thinking and acting. To conceive of faculty development as less than increased *complexity*— and thus possibly increased tension and concern over one's role and responsibilities—will lead to inadequate programs for assisting faculty growth. These programs must be based on an understanding of personality development as a whole, not just on adapting to a professional role. Toward this end, this paper describes a scheme of stages of faculty development.

As is the case with any scientific construct, the origins of this developmental progression scheme were theoretical and empirical. Although the first conception of faculty as developing adults was formulated by my associates Robert Shukraft and J. Wesley Brown, my plan developed along somewhat different theoretical lines, using as a point of departure the work of such developmental theorists as Loevinger and Wessler (1970) and Perry (1970).

The unique aspect of their work is that they examine the form or structure of an individual's assumptions about social reality and how these change through life. Development means dealing with experience in increasingly sophisticated and complex ways and being able to integrate this complexity into stable structures. The focus here is not on the content of development—the specific issues that preoccupy an individual at a given time in life—but the structures he uses to generate that content. As Kohlberg and Gilligan note (1971), such theories look at *how* an individual thinks about such matters as good and bad, or truth and beauty, but not *what* he thinks about at any given time.

With this general point of view in mind I examined the protocols of the interviews that our research team had carried out with faculty members at one large state university. These interviews covered such matters as personal and educational background, views on teaching, students, and colleagues, and their professional goals. The questions were open-ended and faculty were encouraged to respond fully and freely.

With these data I ordered faculty along a continuum according to the complexity and generality of the assumptions which underlay the meaning they gave to their professional lives. I analyzed their views concerning the process of education, including their conception of the nature of knowledge and their philosophy of teaching; their notions of their roles as professors; their relation to their discipline; and their attitudes toward others, both colleagues and students.

The continuum portrays a progression from a position where faculty see knowledge as an unambiguous entity, and where teaching consists of simply presenting facts to students, to a position where they begin to see knowledge in more differentiated terms and recognize the need to use various strategies to help students gain understanding. Farther along the progression is a more problematic notion of knowledge, accompanied by a view of teaching as helping the student develop frameworks for ordering unrelated facts, to impose order on chaos, as it were. The concept of professional role evolves from simple definitions of right and wrong actions, to an awareness of choice in roles and a sense of possible restrictions and limitations, and finally to a sense of style and tolerance within their choice of roles. In relations with others the progression goes from a view of people in moralistic terms of good and bad, to a more psychologically insightful notion of people that recognizes the origins of manipulation and inequality in human relations, and then to a sense of commitment in a context of tolerance and reciprocity.

After sorting faculty along this continuum I grouped them into five levels or stages. The five stages of the developmental scheme are as follows.

stage one

At this level the faculty member has a simple view of his role and the nature of his work. His professional reference group provides his role definition, and he enacts it in conventional fashion. Thus, in a large university he might see himself in terms of what is expected of a member of his academic discipline, while at a small college he might adopt local conventions. Similarly, he defines educational goals in accord with his reference group and may even believe that training new recruits for his profession is the sole aim of education. His goals are distinguished by their rather stereotyped form rather than their specific content. Knowledge is absolute and given; education consists of pouring facts into an empty vessel, the student, who assimilates a body of knowledge. His views of students, grading procedures, and the like are relatively undifferentiated. There are right and wrong procedures, and they may be easily catalogued. Grading reflects the degree to which students know right from wrong information. His opinions are rather dogmatic and are distinguished by their lack of complexity. Their presentation tends to preclude argument and alternative points of view. For this kind of professor the world is divided into areas of good and bad by some authority, usually his reference group. Conventionality, perhaps banality, dominates his professional life. He probably finds campus change very perplexing because he has not evolved suf-

64

ficiently complex cognitive schemata to cope with them. Sixteen percent of the sample were in Stage One.

stage two

The professor in this stage has a more complex notion of his role than does his Stage-One colleague. He may still define his role in relation to conventional reference groups, but he demonstrates increasing distance from them. Nonetheless, the certainty of right action as derived from authority is never in doubt. His view of knowledge is gaining in complexity. Although the aim continues to be the acquisition of facts by students, this faculty member is interested in helpful techniques. The nature and source of knowledge are clear, but one must find the right methods for presenting them. He still sees people in monolithic good and bad terms, but now he is willing to try to explain their behavior, usually in terms of simple causal relationships—for example, between behavior and social class or behavior and childhood experience. This professor has had some experience with diverse opinions, with views contrary to his own, and so his position is relatively articulate. Twenty-one percent of my sample were in Stage Two.

stage three

The faculty member is further distant from reference-group definitions of his role. He has a heightened consciousness of choice and is therefore aware of possible limitations of his freedom. He may display some anxiety as a result of trying to synthesize disparate elements in his role. This individual has considerable psychological insight into interpersonal relations: he can see students and colleagues in terms of inner motives and their relation to behavior. As an educator he seeks to create conditions in which students may learn, and he believes they can learn only by active effort. This faculty member adheres to a problematic idea of knowledge. At this stage his philosophy of education may appear to be permissive. His ability to think in psychological terms and his appreciation of human variousness contribute to a heightened sense of responsibility and conscientiousness. Although he is more open to choice and diversity than are his less-developed compatriots, he has not integrated these elements. Sixteen percent were in this stage.

The prototypic faculty member of Stage Four not only has a sense of freedom and relativity in social roles, he has evolved a personal style of functioning. He has mastered some role conflicts and has achieved partial synthesis. He is liberated from the excessive conscientiousness that at times characterizes the faculty member in Stage Three. He has a sense of reciprocity in human relations and education: he believes a faculty member should not only give but get. He enjoys people, in contrast to those in Stage Three, who seem preoccupied by the possibility of manipulation and inequality in human relationships. Learning is the ability to synthesize, not just soak up, diverse facts and information. Students must discover answers for themselves. At this stage the professor can readily see things from the students' side. The permissiveness which sometimes appeared in Stage Three has been replaced by a slightly more structured view which still values the autonomy of the student. Synthesis among diversity and complexity is stressed. Twenty-one percent of my sample fit in here.

stage five

At this stage the faculty member has a more clearly articulated position than does his colleague of Stage Four. For example, included in his philosophy of education is explicit concern with helping students develop a sense of values or character. He has a real appreciation of the student's situation and how material may best be learned. Not only has he realized the reciprocity of Stage Four, he is able to find satisfaction in relationships with students of whom he may be critical. This tolerance is a conscious or explicit construct; he is aware, that is, of having developed a sense of tolerance, an ability to live with diversity. Considerable cognitive complexity is evident at this stage. The prototypic faculty member is able to accept contradiction and ambivalence in human functioning and irony in social processes and to carry on effectively within such contexts. Individuals who reached this stage constitute 26 percent of my sample.

validation

In developing typologies, it is customary (and considered acceptable) to stop at the point we have now reached—the level of theory generation. I believed, however, that we had to move beyond generation to validation. If the scheme was valid, there should be a high level of agreement among raters using the scheme. I therefore asked three psychologists to rate interviews of faculty members from a small state college. (This second sample, from a different type of institution, was used in order to provide the most powerful test of the scheme's generality.) The level of agreement for Kendall's coefficient of concordance (w) (Siegel, 1956) was .80, which was converted into an average Spearman rank correlation coefficient of .70 ($p < .001$). The level of agreement among the three raters was such that comparable results would occur by chance less than one time in a thousand.

further considerations and implications

Loevinger (1966) states that a developmental model has the following characteristics: (1) there is an invariable order of the stages of development; (2) no stage can be skipped; (3) each stage is more complex than the preceding one; and (4) each stage is based on the preceding one and prepares for the succeeding one. I believe the scheme I have presented is fully developmental in this sense, except for one limitation: faculty members may be located at stages higher than One or Two without having passed through them in their earlier professional careers. In some cases there is evidence that they passed through these first stages when they were graduate students or even undergraduates. For example, we found in several interviews retrospective accounts of faculty who had experienced development according to the scheme.

These stages do not encompass the whole of ego development as conceived by Loevinger and Wessler (1970). I am concerned with ego development only as it relates to a professor's professional development, as expressed in such aspects of his life as his career, his teaching, his views of students and colleagues, and his ideas about the nature of knowledge. One would expect, of course, some correlation between professional growth and ego development as more generally conceived, and in fact the modal ratings in my second (state-college) sample correlate .28 with the Loevinger Sentence Completion Test (Loevinger and Wessler, 1970), a measure of ego development.

In light of this developmental scheme, can we find out which experiences have the most favorable impact on development? We should consider the point of Loevinger and Wessler: ego structures are relatively stable entities; they change only slowly. The professional development of professors, a facet of their ego development, is such a structure and is not easily modified. Development occurs when the individual is confronted with novel perspectives and events that he cannot account for with his usual assumptions. The integration of this new experience must occur slowly if the stability of the ego is to be maintained. If change is too rapid, this security is threatened. If nothing else, development is an intensely personal thing, and rightly so. The individual best knows the rate of growth consistent with his or her stability. Changing faculty in important ways is difficult, and the types of experiences that are likely to have an impact would have to be intense and yet carried out with care and sensitivity.*

It might seem natural to assume that the more developed a professor is, the better teacher he will be. In something as complex as student-teacher interaction, however, no simple global statement about what makes a good teacher is possible. We must ask "Good for what?" and "Good for whom?" before any broad statement can be made. There are many possible criteria for defining a good teacher. Is such a judgment to be made by student evaluations, by other faculty, by administrators, by measuring student gains in knowledge or ability to think critically, or by studies of the careers of former students? All of these are plausible means, yet each has limitations. It is interesting to note that when Gaff and Wilson (1971) compared faculty selected as outstanding teachers with a random sample they found "that nominated faculty did not differ from their nonnominated colleagues in a statistically significant way." One explanation offered for this finding was that no one trait accounts for good teaching—it rests on multiple sources.

What, then, is the significance of faculty development in the terms I have described? I believe that it provides a model which transcends the notion of faculty development as mere adjustment or acquiesence to roles with a minimum of stress. The model presents a course of growth that offers professors ever-greater choice

*Morimoto (1971) attempts to influence Harvard teaching fellows by means of groups that include both didactic and experiential elements. In these groups basic assumptions about people and instruction are examined in a spirit of free and nonthreatening inquiry.

68

and complexity in constructing their roles. Further, I believe that the greater the faculty member's development the greater his or her potential for helping students increase their own growth. In an age that seems to become increasingly turbulent and bewildering, more complex and humane ways of thinking and valuing are essential steps in a person's development.

references

Gaff, J. G., and Wilson, R. C. *The Teaching Environment: A Study of Optimum Working Conditions for Effective College Teaching.* Berkeley: The Center for Research and Development in Higher Education, University of California, June 1971.

Kohlberg, L., and Gilligan, C. "The Adolescent As Philosopher: The Description of Self in a Post-Conventional World." *Daedalus,* 1971, *100*(4), 1015-1086.

Loevinger, J. "The Meaning and Measure of Ego Development." *American Psychologist,* 1966, *21*, 195-206.

Loevinger, J., and Wessler, R. *Measuring Ego Development.* San Francisco: Jossey-Bass, 1970.

Morimoto, K. "Supervising Teachers in Groups." Cambridge: Harvard Bureau of Study Counsel, August 1971, mimeographed.

Perry, W. *Forms of Intellectual and Ethical Development during the College Years.* New York: Holt, Rinehart, and Winston, 1970.

Siegel, S. *Non Parametric Statistics for the Behavioral Sciences.* New York: McGraw-Hill Book Co. Inc., 1956.

Adaptation to innovative colleges may be difficult, but if faculty can cope it may help them become more developed teachers.

innovative colleges: challenge to faculty development

norbert ralph
mervin freedman

In studying college faculty for the past three years, we have been particularly fascinated with their adaptation to innovative colleges.* Despite the great diversity among these colleges, we have been struck time and again by the similar problems faced by their faculties. The movement from traditional to innovative educational settings creates a crisis in faculty development. (We use the word *crisis*, as does Erikson, 1969, to refer to a period of heightened potential and vulnerability.) We have seen hope followed shortly by despair, remarkable growth coupled with startling regression, and the like—

*By *innovative college*, we do not refer to every new or experimental program in any college anywhere, but to a subset of this group: those sharing the innovative model of education defined below. Further, even though we have seen the innovative model in educational settings ranging from high schools to graduate schools, we are referring to the modal case of a four-year experimental cluster college.

all due to the fundamental necessity of adapting to drastic change. Faculty participation in an experimental college experience may enlarge the sense of choice and competence or it may result in loss of self-esteem and a sense of failure. Thus, innovation seems to be by nature an imprecise art fraught with uncertainty and anxiety.

In this article we analyze how similar conditions create a common set of problems for faculty in innovative colleges. We examine interrelated phenomena at three levels: the societal, the organizational, and the individual. As part of this analysis we consider some characteristics of an innovative model of education; the kind of social environment that develops in experimental colleges; the impact of an innovative environment on faculty; how professors have adapted to this environment; and finally, the future of alternative educational forms.

the innovative model

Faculty members become committed to innovative colleges largely because of their dissatisfaction with traditional forms of higher education.* This dissatisfaction commonly becomes crystallized over specific extraeducational issues, when campuswide disruptions such as the Berkeley Free Speech Movement or the Cambodia crisis throw into question assumptions on which conventional higher education is based. In this turbulent climate faculty explicitly address fundamental educational issues which had been only on the periphery of their awareness. They are no longer certain that traditional approaches can prepare students to cope effectively with rapid social change.

People must learn to deal with a culture in which change and turbulence are the only constants, in which the authority of conventional concepts of social reality is no more and individuals are confronted with the relativity of all such constructs. Under these conditions, the new educational task is to help individuals make commitments in a new kind of social field. One college founder

*A more detailed discussion would include ideas about the types of faculty who are attracted to and selected by innovative colleges. We have research to show that ideologically and characterologically they are different from parent-college faculty. Dr. Lynnette Beall has also suggested that faculty could be divided into conflicted and conflict-free innovators. Such a discussion is beyond the scope of our concerns here, however.

describes the situation succinctly: "An awareness of basic premises, a formulation of integrating patterns or world views, is one of contemporary man's most urgent needs." As he put it, a college is successful to the extent that it can "replace meaninglessness with significance and estrangement with communion." A new educational form is needed because by its very structure traditional education may perpetuate maladaptation.

The innovative model of education is seen as a solution to the deficiencies of traditional education, which is seen as disciplinary, authoritative, and academic. In contrast, the innovative model is interdisciplinary, egalitarian, and developmental. An interdisciplinary approach is needed because the usual separation of the domains of knowledge fosters only partial solutions to complex contemporary problems; these require methods of inquiry that cut across conventional academic fields. This aspect of the model calls for members of different disciplines to work together, often using a team-teaching approach.

Power and decision-making originate from an egalitarian rather than an authoritative* base. That is, no element of the social structure is considered as given by authority, whether this be a professor, a discipline, or a tradition. For example, evaluation procedures and curriculum, usually defined only by faculty in traditional academic settings, are to be arrived at by consensus among all constituents of the college. Consensus thus emerges from this egalitarian orientation as the most appropriate mode of governance.

Egalitarianism also characterizes personal relations between faculty and students. While in conventional programs faculty are viewed as authorities to be treated with a certain amount of respect and deference, in innovative colleges their position is more like that of a peer. To emphasize this distinction, faculty are often referred to as "resource people" or "co-learners," peers in the search for knowledge.

*In attempting to describe the power dimension of the traditional model of education we tried to find a word which would convey the idea that the exercise of power in that frame of reference could have a legitimate basis. In that context the professor wields power on the basis of personal expertise and competence; presumably he is able to make judgments on educational issues with more competence than students. The word *authoritative* seemed the best choice. *Authoritarian* was another possibility, but we wished to reserve this term for the exercise of power in an irrational manner, that is, for power not based on competence and exercised illegitimately.

The educational goal most frequently stated is to promote the growth and development of the individual as a personal and social being. While the traditional mode stresses the acquisition of certain facts, techniques, or vocational abilities, from the innovative perspective the primary task is to acquire a more general set of skills which might be called learning how to learn, thus to become an autonomous learner who is flexible enough to adapt to a fast-changing environment. This goal will be accomplished most easily when students are intrinsically motivated, when they have wide latitude to realize themselves. Any hierarchical or formal structural arrangements are undesirable, since they provide an individual with something·less than complete freedom and autonomy for growth.* The faculty member's primary function is not dispensing information but rather serving the more global aim of promoting character development—both the student's and his own.

the innovative environment

The social environments within the innovative colleges we studied† were highly unusual and quite unlike what the founding faculty had expected. Since students and faculty come to these colleges because of a strong dissatisfaction with traditional forms, they are determined not to create another structure which would perpetuate old ills. As a result, remnants of traditional models are abandoned with a vengeance in the early stages of these colleges. Highly structured forms of evaluation such as tests and grading are dropped, along with standard curricula and conventional roles. Traditional academic goals are little valued; they may even be regarded as handicaps to student development. In this beginning period community identity is to a large extent negatively defined. Being

---

*The developmental theory implicit here is close to what Kohlberg and Mayer (1972) describe as romanticism: "Romantics hold that what comes from within the child is the most important aspect of development; therefore the pedagogical environment should be permissive enough to allow the inner 'good' to unfold and the inner 'bad' to come under control. Teaching the child the ideas and attitudes of others through rote or drill would result in meaningless learning and the suppression of inner spontaneous tendencies of positive value." The romantic view of development is to be distinguished from a progressive theory which Kohlberg and Mayer hold to be the only viable model.

†For a highly descriptive and rich study of similar types of experimental colleges, see Jerome (1971).

innovative means being antitraditional, antiacademic, and anti-authority.

Though traditional structures are easily abandoned, new ones are established only with great difficulty, for several reasons. First, there is a tendency to view the creation of any structures as a regression to a traditional model—since the old way was highly organized, being without structure is seen as a virtue. Second, since decision-making is by consensus, all details of curriculum, evaluation, admissions procedures, faculty-student roles, use of resources, and the like have to be decided by long and arduous group discussions of the town-meeting variety. The time and turmoil connected with reaching something that feels like consensus are probably unrivaled in the life of other organizations. For example, in one college we studied, it took three weeks of meeting every day for three hours to arrive at an evaluation procedure that everyone could accept. (One irony of these colleges is that their decision-making process is inherently conservative because of this egalitarian style of governance. Everyone has a chance to veto procedures or at least delay consensus, and there is likely to be at least one person who finds some reason to do so.)

A third reason for the difficulty in building new forms is that administrative energies are likely to be focused on resolving the reciprocal antagonisms and stereotyping between the parent college and the innovative college—trying to explain the new college to the parent administration, board of trustees, evaluating committees, and the surrounding community and, similarly, to explain the actions of these bodies to members of the innovative college. Little time or energy is left for developing internal procedures and structures. Because of these factors, old forms are often eliminated without new ones taking their place.

Another irony is that innovative colleges, founded with the hope of replacing "meaninglessness with significance and estrangement with communion," tend to heighten feelings of meaninglessness and estrangement at the beginning, as the participants struggle to develop open-ended, individually defined models for education. The turbulence and anomie that characterize the larger social system are present in an intensified form in this environment, accentuating alienation among members of the college community.

In this early period the college is virtually a community without a social structure. Unless it can move beyond this stage, it fails

to provide for certain basic needs. In our view the primary psychological need satisfied by social structures is to provide an individual
with well-defined and socially sanctioned paths of action for maintaining a sense of security and self-esteem. When such structures are
lacking, as happens frequently in the case of innovative colleges,
individuals experience loss of self-esteem and increased anxiety. A
major determinant of organizational structure is the need to find
socially defined and shared defenses against these feelings.

impact on faculty

Our studies reveal that faculty who come to innovative colleges are quite unprepared for this environment. The profound discontinuity between a conventional setting and this one produces a
kind of culture shock. Most everyone feels disappointed and de-
ceived at some level, especially the minority of tradition-oriented
faculty who, because of the ambiguous image of the innovative
college, imagined they could pursue standard academic goals with
merely a few new innovative wrinkles. Antagonism between these
faculty members and the more radical majority of the college community is often severe and a source of constant conflict. However,
all faculty, regardless of their initial expectations, tend to be sur-
prised. No matter what they were told, they usually expect something fairly familiar and comfortable that coincides with their own
patterns and values. One faculty member told us:

> I expected the program to be a challenging, active in-
> tellectual pursuit of an interdisciplinary theme with the stu-
> dents actively contributing to the inquiry. I also expected
> that the students would respond to the self-initiated dimen-
> sion of the program and begin looking into issues that con-
> cerned them. A line from *Hair* goes, "When he [LBJ] got
> there, what did he see—the youth of America on LSD." In-
> stead of intellectually curious students I found gripers . . .
> con-men, escapists from the regular school, the "easy riders,"
> fifteen-units-for-doing-nothing anarchists, any structure is
> bad, rampant antiintellectualism, students handicapped by
> reading ability and interest. In short, I was expecting too
> much of the students: why should this program attract any
> different population from the regular college? . . . we entered

the experimental college with our own private hopes for an exciting educational experience. Unfortunately, these hopes were developed prior to actual engagement with the reality of the program and therefore were private fantasies.

In the early stages faculty find it difficult to make an accurate assessment of how unfamiliar the setting actually is. Despite intentions to the contrary, most continue to teach in fairly standard ways. They want to give up conventional roles, but in some ways these roles, which habitually provided them with a certain sense of security and self-esteem, work better than the new and very uncertain arrangements. But once faculty confront the fact that half-way modifications of a traditional approach are not really so innovative as they and their students wish, they are faced with a frightening prospect: changing their behavior to accommodate the novel conditions of the college.*

To change in such important ways is always difficult. Eric Hoffer (1963, p. 3) has written incisively on the concept of change: "We can never be really prepared for that which is wholly new. We have to adjust ourselves, and every radical adjustment is a crisis in self-esteem; we undergo a test, we have to prove ourselves. It needs inordinate self-confidence to face drastic change without inner trembling."

To a considerable degree faculty have been socialized by their discipline. Suddenly, they must teach from another perspective, often with a teacher from another field in a team arrangement. The result is a multidisciplinary approach rather than a truly interdisciplinary one, leaving students with the work of real synthesis—a job which often generates a good deal of complaint. Developing interdisciplinary teaching skills, like acquiring any other new and difficult skill, is a challenge. A faculty member commented, "We spent interminable hours in faculty meetings trying to coordinate our efforts to focus on the theme. We were beginning to really

*What individuals want is never a simple matter, and especially so in this case. It is probably more accurate to state that the desire of a majority of students and faculty for a radically innovative college is ambivalent. For example, some students want initially to be totally free to do whatever they choose, but soon became anxious about taking responsibility for this freedom and demand guidance from faculty. Faculty, trying to extend help to students, then may be rebuffed in subtle ways—reinforcing the students' and their own ambivalence.

understand for the first time the concept of interdisciplinary teaching. It was still a new behavior to work through."

The most fundamental change to which faculty must adjust is the abandonment of their role as authorities in favor of a more egalitarian stance. In traditional settings faculty are able to structure evaluation procedures and curriculum according to their own needs and interests, but in the innovative college, where students needs and interests are given first priority, faculty are no longer masters of their own fate; they are very much at the mercy of the whims of students. Some faculty find sharing authority with students so unacceptable that they withdraw from the program. Others want to avoid the appearance of being authoritarian, and they lean over backward to do so. But in avoiding the Scylla of authoritarianism, they may veer toward the Charybdis of the opposite pole.

Even those faculty who accept the need for more egalitarian relationships are unprepared, on the one hand, for the hostile frankness of many students in this rather rebellious setting or, on the other, for the lack of distance from students and their needs. In programs that require students to depart from conventional roles, they are often thrust into periods of intense crisis, and frequently faculty are called on to help them not only with educational matters but with a variety of personal issues, some of them highly charged emotionally. The problem is especially acute for faculty in residential programs, where students expect them to be on call twenty-four hours a day. One group of faculty stated that they had the feeling of being "cannibalized." Their involvement with students is so exhausting and time-consuming that they have little time or energy for their own private lives and their intellectual or research activities.

It is also a new experience for faculty to teach with developmental rather than purely academic goals in mind. In traditional settings faculty have some idea of what academic achievement means and also how to evaluate it with grades. But how to create teaching methods that will produce character development, refinement of personal sensibilities and values, independent judgment, flexible perspectives, and the like is a mystery to faculty. Obviously teaching with a concern for the personal development of students entails much experimentation and inevitably some failures.

Evaluating students according to developmental goals provokes some of the most bitter disputes in innovative colleges, not only because these goals are hard to define but also because of consensual decision-making. As a result, faculty tend to let the question of evaluation slide until the end of a semester or the approach of graduation requires that it be directly faced. At this point antagonistic positions concerning goals for the college become explicit. Without some appropriate mechanisms to resolve these disputes, they become protracted, and some faculty choose to leave the program at this time as a consequence.

In summary, faculty members find adaptation far more challenging than they had expected. Their new role requires that they learn to serve as facilitators rather than authorities. They must help students derive their own goals rather than imposing them. Instead of prescribing certain information to be learned, they must assist students in finding out what needs to be known. By being routinely presented with issues on which they are not experts yet which students wish to explore, faculty begin to serve as models of the learning process as they show students how they themselves research novel problems. This type of learning may be the most valuable, as Michael Polanyi (1958) notes: "By watching his master and emulating his efforts in the presence of his example the apprentice unconsciously picks up the rules of an art, including those which are not explicitly known to the master himself." But this role is difficult for some faculty. A student commented, "This kind of educational experience, which requires that a student learn as much from what a teacher *is* as from what he *says*, is very threatening to some."

Confronted with these many demands, most faculty feel bewildered and at times severely threatened. Some find it necessary to leave, as we mentioned earlier; others who stay on find the emotional price quite high, and psychological and somatic difficulties often ensue. A few individuals who have great self-confidence and little investment in traditional roles are able to fare well in the program. The initial period of innovation and experiment is often full of intensity and excitement. To venture into the unknown, to try something new, is frightening but also thrilling. It is to define oneself, at least for a time, as incompetent according to long-held values.

faculty adaptation and development

Most educational innovations are incremental in nature, and the adjustments faculty have to make are correspondingly small.

But innovative colleges are a qualitatively different educational milieu. Their discontinuity with traditional settings is so great that faculty have to create genuinely new models with little personal experience or educational tradition to serve as bases. However, the turmoil, the sense of discovery, the feelings of community, and the intimacy can be valuable and cherished experiences. As one professor recalls: "Even though the program was exhausting it was more stimulating and exciting than my courses in the regular traditional program. I liked the family-community feeling the group generated. I liked many of the people in the program. It was a very human place to be."

With the passage of time faculty members begin to acquire new skills in performing their roles. They develop the capacity for interdisciplinary approaches to intellectual problems. They learn to place realistic but sympathetic limits on the emotional demands which students make. They become sensitive to the character-developing functions of teaching and to personal development as well as academic achievement.

Some faculty find ways to give students guidance and evaluation even when there are no structures to validate such feedback. For example, at times students may define goals for themselves that are unrealistic, or they may approach a subject in a limited or shallow manner. On these occasions, even though faculty find them difficult, straight talk and clear, explicit evaluation are desirable. In our interviews students frequently criticized faculty for holding back on such evaluation: lack of frank criticism not only denied them the opportunity to experience faculty as three-dimensional people, it also short-circuited an important part of their process of self-definition. As Sanford has noted: "Freshmen flourish best not when they are given no grades, but when they are given searching and hard-hitting analyses of their performances—accompanied by intelligible and realistic pictures of what they can become" (1962, p. 264).

Most important of all, as a result of the innovative experience, many faculty members become more developed teachers. By *developed* we do not mean simply becoming a more skillful teacher; we mean that faculty have a more differentiated view of their role. For example, several teachers said that when they returned to traditional settings they had at their disposal not only conventional techniques but more experimental ones too, and they could use either as appropriate. Faculty in innovative settings have to read more widely and think more broadly than they would in usual teaching situations because of the interdisciplinary thrust of their programs. Experimental colleges give them experience with a range of possibilities in education that most teachers can only read about. One teacher commented:

> The college gave me firsthand experience with alternative educational programs and tempered my educational idealism with reality. Keeping intellectual company with the critics and prophets of education doesn't work when you have to deal with individuals who have not been exposed to these points of view—educators, teachers, students. Before I came to the college, I conducted some classes on an open, minimum-requirement basis with somewhat disastrous results; I think I believed too blindly in a method or approach to education and lacked enough actual experience with such a method in operation to avoid the pitfalls.

One important factor that helps faculty improve their skills is that the program as a whole gains coherence and stability as it proceeds. It acquires a more substantial culture, a set of structures and procedures that become routinized and a set of symbols with which individuals can identify and which permit joint action and joint understanding. One faculty member recalls an element of this process: "In the third semester a list of undebatables was developed so as to indicate that the program had elements that were essential to the experiment. This minimized the endless dialogue."

As time passes, conflict between the innovative program and the parent institution is likely to diminish. Less energy is invested in self-justification and defense against hostile criticism and more in the actual operation of the program. Although uncertainty concerning course content and evaluation may remain, reduced antagonism and scrutiny by the parent institution enable the innovative college to progress in self-definition.

Another factor permitting the development of an innovative culture and laying the groundwork for coherent faculty roles is the fact that the highly turbulent, frustration-filled climate of the 1960s has gradually settled into calm, perhaps even apathy. Innovative colleges, consequently, may operate within a less charged milieu. This relatively stable setting permits faculty to develop a more secure and comfortable role for themselves and the skills that go with it.

continuing issues

The problem of how to foster both developmental goals and traditional academic objectives is a prickly one for the faculty. As we have said, innovative programs are likely to avoid defining educational goals in the usual academic fashion. Affective and interpersonal growth and general character development take precedence over intellectual or professional achievement. The faculty must find ways to integrate the innovative and the traditional. Loevinger observes that the separation of development into affective and cognitive spheres is probably "a relic of outworn categories of thought, for integration of observations into a coherent frame of reference is obviously cognitive, while anxiety is obviously affective. But the failure to attain a meaningful and coherent integration is precisely what generates anxiety" (Loevinger and Wessler, 1970, p. 8).

A related issue is the success of these programs in preparing students for engagement in "real life." If developmental goals are emphasized rather than vocational and professional ones, where does this leave students after they graduate? Will they be able to compete with graduates of traditional colleges for jobs and for entrance into graduate schools? Some students in innovative colleges find it hard to leave and want to prolong their stay. Others conclude that their only choice for postgraduate work is a so-called experimental graduate program. Faculty often have the nagging feeling that innovative colleges prepare students just as poorly for engagement with important life tasks as do traditional schools.

future innovation

Educational innovation entails introducing change into a social system. Menzies (1960, p. 108) comments:

Change is inevitably to some extent an excursion into the unknown. It implies a commitment to future events that are not entirely predictable, and to their consequences, and inevitably provokes doubt and anxiety. Any significant change within a social system implies changes in existing social relationships and in social structure. It follows that any significant social change implies a change in the operation of the social system as a defense system. While this change is proceeding, i.e., while social defenses are being restructured, anxiety is likely to be more open and intense. Jaques (1955) has stressed that resistance to social change can better be understood if it is seen as the resistance of groups of people unconsciously clinging to existing institutions because changes threaten existing social defenses against deep and intense anxieties.

In her remarks, we find two important considerations for educational change. First, innovators must be aware that some of their expectations of these programs will inevitably be frustrated. Faculty who have a large emotional investment in the initial plans will tend to resist adaptation. But any persons engaged in social innovation must learn to continually reevaluate early formulations in the light of unanticipated consequences. Likewise, faculty recruiters should admit to the uncertainty. They frequently give potential instructors an optimistic view of the program which ignores the negative features, and such recruits, eager to find a situation congruent with their ideals, are likely to enter into this mutual deception.

Second, organizational change cannot occur unless real people, (not manipulable elements in someone's ideal plan) change their behavior. While the individual is creating a new role and identity, anxiety and conflict are to be expected, but there should be ways of eliminating unnecessary stress so that the experience can be integrated into his personality, giving the person an enlarged sense of choice and competence.

references

Erikson, E. H. *Identity: Youth and Crisis*. New York: Norton, 1969.
Hainer, R. "Rationalism, Pragmatism, and Existentialism: Perceived But Undiscovered Multicultural Problems." In E. Glatt and M. Shelly (Eds.), *The Research Society*. New York: Gordon and Breveh Science Publications, 1968.
Hoffer, E. *The Ordeal of Change*. New York: Harper, 1963.
Jerome, J. *Culture Out of Anarchy*. New York: Herder & Herder, 1971.
Keniston, K. "Youth, Change, and Violence." *American Scholar*, 1968, 37(2).

Kohlberg, L., and Mayer, R. "Development as the Aim of Education." *Harvard Educational Review*, 1972, *42*(4).

Loevinger, J., and Wessler, R. *Measuring Ego Development 1*. San Francisco: Jossey-Bass, 1970.

Menzies, I. E. P. "A Case-Study in the Functioning of Social Systems as a Defense Against Anxiety." *Human Relations*, 1960, *13*(2).

Polanyi, M. *Personal Knowledge*. Chicago: University of Chicago Press, 1958.

Sanford, N. (Ed.) *The American College: A Psychological and Sociological Interpretation of Higher Learning*. New York: Wiley, 1962.

Steps colleges are taking to facilitate their
faculty members' continued development as
institutional needs and priorities change

institutional approaches
to faculty development

donald r. gerth

The phrase *faculty development* has some unfortunate connotations. To many it hints of antiprofessionalism, perhaps even anti-intellectualism. Just as few people wish to be colonized, not many faculty want to be developed. By suggesting they need improvement, the phrase seems to indicate that faculty lack quality or competence. Perhaps *faculty support* or *faculty growth* would be happier labels. Yet any impartial and thoughtful observer of higher education will clearly identify the need for some kind of aid to faculty, perhaps even a survival plan for a few.

The purpose of faculty development, no matter what name it has, is to strengthen faculty members' capacity to work with students and to keep up with expanding knowledge of their field. As part of this overall goal, faculty should learn how to apply technological tools to instruction and to work beyond narrowly defined specializations.

interest in development

Why is faculty development coming to the forefront now, when higher education has less public support and may be under more attack than at any time in our history? In part, the question

83

contains the answer: as Freedman and Sanford indicated earlier in this issue, faculty are less secure and have less to be secure about. Other answers lie in new modes of instruction and in the fact that a period of unparalleled growth in higher education is coming to an end. Great universities and small colleges as late as World War II lived with relatively fixed faculty populations; but over the past twenty-five years they developed new patterns of staffing based on constant institutional expansion. As programs grew in size, individual faculty specialization also increased. Now, institutions and their faculty will have to readjust to comparative stability.

This article reports on these issues from the vantage point of one academic administrator whose institution is grappling with them and who is therefore inquisitive about activities at other institutions.*

Over the summer of 1972, administrative officers and faculty leaders at the California State University at Chico began to review its policies regarding faculty development in light of a new academic master plan then being implemented. To provide some comparative information, it seemed a good idea to look at what was happening elsewhere. We knew that a number of institutions around the country were addressing the issue of faculty development, but when we inquired about their programs, we learned that discussion and planning were far more common than actual programs. A few institutions, however, were actively concerned with faculty growth through systematic support, and several of them were experimenting with growth contracts as part of their programs. Knowing about their efforts should be useful to other institutions, just as it has been to Chico.

hampshire college

Hampshire College, the experimental private liberal arts college that opened in Amherst, Massachusetts, in 1970, operates without faculty tenure. Faculty members are appointed initially for three or four years and may be reappointed thereafter for a period of up to seven years. An initial appointment is based on the col-

*I wish to thank Vice-President Ralph C. Atkinson, Jr., of Ottawa University, Dean Robert C. Birney of Hampshire College, Assistant to the President Richard Chait of Stockton State College, and many colleagues at Chico for their useful information and inputs.

lege's broad definition of the particular faculty position, after which the new faculty member reaches an agreement with his (or her) dean and another faculty colleague that defines his specific role and indicates what will reasonably be expected of him. This "growth contract" includes duties, expectations, responsibilities, accountability, and academic privileges. Subsequently, the dean collects evaluative materials in a file open to the faculty member, information which is used in an annual verbal review of the contract.

If the faculty member wishes to continue at Hampshire, the first contract is renegotiated beginning at least nineteen months before its expiration. It is up to the individual instructor to begin this process himself by writing a proposal about what he plans to do in the new contract period, including such commitments as courses to be taught, participation in program development, and field study or research that might include students. Ultimately, if reappointment for up to another seven years occurs, a new growth contract agreement is reached between the faculty member and the college based on this proposal.

This approach thus provides regular evaluation of all faculty, mutual and periodic agreement on expectations, and assistance in continuous growth. The faculty member enjoys the initiative of asking for a renegotiation of the conditions of the contract at any time, and may request assistance of Hampshire's Office of Institutional Research and Evaluation in developing his skills to meet these conditions. By this and less formal means, Hampshire is striving to provide inservice development for its faculty; and when an individual's contract is not renewed, the college helps to place him at another institution.

ottawa university

Ottawa University, a small Baptist college in Ottawa, Kansas, has recently been undertaking widespread revisions and innovations in its program. Yet its faculty situation is quite stable: nearly 80 percent have tenure, and thus the university has sought effective strategies for stimulating professional growth. Three years ago it developed its own program by allocating twenty thousand dollars to allow twenty faculty members—a third of the total group—to participate in a summer workshop in preparation for launching a new interdisciplinary general education program. Each participant was reimbursed for participating in the workshop, which involved preparation of the course syllabus, setting objectives, and instruction in the teaching process.

Results of this initial session proved so encouraging that Ottawa obtained a grant from the National Endowment for the Humanities to conduct additional workshops for the rest of the faculty. For three weeks in the summer of 1971 and 1972, faculty members focused on group dynamics and interpersonal communication in the teaching process and within their own ranks. Ottawa found these sessions so valuable that it now is using its own funds to continue them for new faculty and for current faculty who are planning new courses.

A parallel part of Ottawa's faculty development program is its experimental evaluation methods that involve goal-setting by the individual faculty member and mutual agreement by the professor and the institution on a growth contract. This growth-oriented approach to faculty assessment employs a "colleague-advisor" system, whereby each faculty member who chooses to participate in the plan discusses his professional goals and strategies with a faculty colleague. The university hopes this approach to faculty appraisal will replace the former system of unilateral evaluations based on reports from department chairmen, faculty, and students; and if this approach is adopted as university policy after its current evaluation, it will be required of all faculty in the future.

This growth contract system is particularly suitable for Ottawa because of its new relationship to its students. Each Ottawa student develops a contract which includes vocational and personal objectives and educational strategies for achieving them. The student's progress toward completing the contract and toward graduation is evaluated by the student, the faculty advisor, course instructors, and ultimately a committee on academic review. Ottawa is testing the proposition that this type of educational planning designed for student growth and development can be adapted to assist faculty as well.

stockton state college

Stockton State College, the two-year-old public college in Pomona, New Jersey, has experienced rapid growth; and having neither the patience nor the crust of tradition, it is exploring new forms of faculty appointment, evaluation, promotion, and tenure within the framework of New Jersey law, which provides for collective bargaining and requires annual reviews of all tenured faculty. As part of its evaluation policies and practices, Stockton has organized annual review conferences for faculty to plan specific developmental objectives; it has created an Office of Academic Development and appointed a dean of academic development, responsible to the academic vice president, to participate in the process of faculty evaluation, review, and development.

New Jersey's new state budget allocated a proportion of faculty salary funds for faculty development; and out of Stockton's 149 budgeted positions this year, only 135 are assigned to direct instruction. Unlike other New Jersey state colleges with a longer history and less flexibility, Stockton is using its remaining positions to permit faculty to plan and revamp courses and programs.

utah state university

The three-year-old Merrill Library and Learning Resources Center at Utah State is providing systematic support to faculty as well as students. One of its four associate directors, Douglas D. Alder, has responsibility for instructional development, while others are in charge of traditional library services, collections development, and the production of films and other instructional media. Alder, a historian who also teaches in Utah State's history department, serves as a consultant on new teaching devices such as television, programmed instruction, and simulation; conducts seminars for faculty on teaching; assists individuals with their teaching; and circulates materials about faculty development. Utah State has been able to create and maintain this program of the Merrill Center on its existing budget, without special outside funding.

Other institutions—among them, the University of Michigan, Michigan State, the University of Tennessee, Northwestern, the University of California at Berkeley—have appointed instructional development officers comparable to Alder at Utah State. And still other colleges are taking different approaches to faculty development. John Noonan of Findlay College in Ohio, for example, describes a design for interinstitutional cooperation in the following article in this issue. How one institution has moved from random efforts at development to a systematic endeavor can be illustrated by recent changes at Chico.

policy at chico

About two years ago the faculty and administration of the California State University at Chico (then Chico State College)—among the oldest of the nineteen state universities and colleges in California—began a searching assessment of the character and quality of the institution and its future. An early decision, made even before declining enrollments became a national concern, was to slow down Chico's growth rate, which had been very high in the 1960s, until the university reached a stabilized size compatible with its modest-sized community and rural setting in the Sacramento Valley. This decision meant that Chico immediately had to consider how it could achieve qualitative growth and a flexible response to changing needs and shifts in enrollments within a context of more or less fixed and stable resources.

Though this situation is not unusual in many fine universities and colleges, for a public institution that has grown fivefold in little more than a decade, it is a marked change. When rapid growth is occurring, plans for new programs, additional faculty, and other changes for the most part assume expansion will continue. Existing resources and faculty activities need not be questioned, and are not. But as soon as they must be examined, some faculty and administrators tend to revert to me-first attitudes about resources: if the university is to top out enrollment by 1975 or 1976, then "my" department or school must get all the resources needed for a mature program now and must maintain or increase its percentage of enrollment and resources until then. How can this competition be reduced and flexibility achieved within a fixed whole?

Out of this discussion, involving both administrative and faculty senate groups, came a proposal based on the assumption that faculty members, as the most important resource of the university, are the key to a flexible response to an uncertain future. In the spring of 1972, the senate presented to the president an Academic Master Plan statement, which asserted that "it is the goal of the university that faculty be open to the development of new competence and expertise and that the university shall encourage and provide for such development." As part of this statement, subsequently approved by the president, these policies were enunciated:

Recruitment procedures shall be oriented toward employment of new faculty with a capacity to adapt their specialities to broader (multiple) rather than narrower (singular) applications. . . .

Universitywide, at least 1 percent of all faculty positions shall be dedicated to faculty development only, not for the administration of the faculty development program. . . . retention, tenure, and promotion procedures are to be planned to encourage faculty academic and professional development and to insure that faculty will receive appropriate consideration for their efforts to adapt to changing modes of instruction and educational demand. . . .

All faculty personnel committees are to be development-oriented. . . .

Innovation in instruction, learning modes, and campus activities shall be encouraged through the establishment of a Faculty Resources Center to include assistance in evaluating classroom teaching behavior, assessing learning and providing resources for development of more effective teaching modes, and incorporating modern instructional media in their programs. . . .

Professional development opportunities are to be afforded each and every faculty member. . . .

The major objectives of the faculty development program shall be the following:

(a) To facilitate faculty developing and maintaining academic and instructional competencies that are valued by the university.

(b) To facilitate for all faculty the maintenance of high standards of teaching, research and scholarly activity, including community service.

(c) To facilitate among all faculty the knowledge of, and capacity to, work with the changing foci of academic programs and modes of instruction within higher education.

(d) To help faculty members broaden their academic and instructional competencies.

This statement called for the creation of "professional development committees" or some other mechanism within each school to guide and implement its own professional development program, instructed every department to devise specific criteria for identifying excellence in teaching, and stated that "in evaluating faculty, excellence in administration, research, and/or services shall not be used to excuse or compensate for a significantly below-average performance in teaching. . . ."

This statement of goals addressed basic institutional needs: flexible response to societal change, new modes of instruction, and qualitative growth of the faculty. So far, so good. But implementation was another matter. Where does one start? Over the summer of 1972, administrative officers and faculty leaders began tackling this always knotty problem, with the knowledge that apprehension about implementation was beginning to appear, particularly among some senior faculty and leaders of at least one faculty organization, who perceived "development" as professionally offensive and potentially manipulative.

implementing policy

Two senior administrators began the process of implementation with a statement to the faculty and department chairmen that "the only colleges and universities that need fear the next twenty years are those that see their present roles so rigidly defined that change is possible only with quantitative growth"; they proposed four general areas of attention: "first, maintaining and developing scholarly competencies that are of value to students, society, and to other faculty members; second, facilitating the highest possible standards of teaching and related activity; third, enlarging the capacity to work with programs changing as the knowledge explosion continues; fourth, broadening our academic and instructional competencies."

Data gathered on faculty characteristics indicated, among other facts, that the median faculty age was under forty (only 22 percent of the faculty were fifty or older) but that 54 percent of the faculty were tenured. A senate committee presented recommendations for implementing a program of faculty "facilitation" that would avoid use of the term *development,* would be totally voluntary on the part of faculty, and would remain separate from the retention, promotion, and tenure review process. As adopted by the faculty senate, the report suggested:

The activities of such a program of faculty facilitation might include, among others, assistance in implementing the presentation of course materials to students, the development of course materials, the utilization of supplemental teaching media, the establishment of course objectives, the evaluation of course outcomes, the preparation of research proposals, the sharpening of research skills, and the development of more adequate student-teacher relationships. Such an effort might best be mounted through utilization of presently existing re sources including media personnel, institutional research personnel, student personnel, office professionals, and teaching colleagues. The administrative contribution might initially be limited to putting faculty with specific needs or interests in touch with others who possess skills relevant to those interests and who are willing to utilize them with others. Should the faculty interest thus identified become sufficiently great, further considerations should then be given to increased resources. The accomplishments of the program should be reviewed at least every two years in order to determine its future.

This report now provides a policy framework within which Chico's efforts to support the enrichment of faculty are being made. Once the administration made clear that support was available, including allocation of resources to faculty members who wished to pursue developmental projects, faculty initiative increased. More than sixty requests for development and innovation reserve funds have already come from a total faculty of some six hundred members. The faculty is now examining the issue of what the percentage of tenured faculty should be in a gradually stabilizing institution.

An associate vice-president for academic affairs has been appointed to coordinate and integrate the library and media services and assist the total enrichment program. This faculty member, skilled in curriculum and learning, is helping individual professors to analyze their instructional objectives and modes as well as to evaluate the teaching-learning process. She is also working with groups of departmental faculty on such projects as the development of blocks of competency courses, self-paced instruction, and self-teaching methods. In addition, using systems analysis, she has helped organize faculty groups to work on campus-supported improvement programs. Perhaps because of the excellence of this individual, other faculty members have begun to seek support—often just moral support—for new projects. This growth in numbers from a few people to a critical mass of faculty indicates that Chico's faculty facilitation movement is well under way.

summing up

Faculty development is important for most, if not all, institutions. The traditional modes of instruction are being displaced by mediated approaches and other unconventional techniques. Institutions are experiencing both increased control from above, in huge statewide systems, and decentralization through community control—however *community* is defined for each institution. And the importance of interdisciplinary work for undergraduates is increasing. Overarching all of these factors is a public call for new sensitivity and responsiveness to students and social need.

Faculty development as it has been discussed at Chico has been perceived by some as a threat or as nonprofessional. But others see it as a response to change, even as a way of actively applying the knowledge we are gaining in the behavioral and social sciences to faculty activities and roles in a culture reassessing its values. It may also be an enlightened survival plan for some instructors. Successful faculty development assumes, implicitly or explicitly, that the faculty is the most important resource of a college or university and therefore that the individual faculty member is not expendable, even when program balance must be shifted or other necessary changes threaten to engulf him.

Donald R. Gerth is professor of political science and vice-president for academic affairs at California State University, Chico. He has been a faculty member at the University of Chicago, Shimer College, and California State University, San Francisco, and has served as associate dean for institutional relations and student affairs of the California State Colleges system. With James O. Haehn and associates he wrote An Invisible Giant: The California State Colleges, *edited* Papers on the Ombudsman in Higher Education, *and coauthored* The Learning Society.

*How faculty members active in experimental courses
can be the nucleus of a faculty development
program, and how their counterparts at neighboring
institutions can play a major role in the program.*

faculty development through experimentation and interinstitutional cooperation

john f. noonan

If colleges and universities planned new programs in the name of faculty change as well as in the name of student change, both groups would be better off. In two recent articles (Noonan, 1971, 1972), I described several alterations in faculty behavior caused by their participation in a variety of yeasty curricular configurations: cluster colleges, problem-centered and interdisciplinary courses, value-oriented and team-taught classes. Despite their high price in anxiety, these new configurations are change-inducing for the faculty who plan and teach them. Surprising as it may sound, faculty are really very much like other people: when you remove them from the way they ordinarily do things and put them in situations where they have to act differently, they sometimes learn. Curricular changes may not deliver all the promises made to students, but they often change faculty more than professors bargain for. If, as many educators now recognize, thrusting students into a new role is an excellent way for students to learn, why won't it work for faculty?

The trouble is that professors are vulnerable in alien learning climates (as Ralph and Freedman pointed out in their earlier article on innovative colleges). They are threatened by the new self-definition required; by substantial investments in time, energy, and worry; by fear of failure; by the unsympathetic attitudes of some colleagues; and by not knowing what to look for as evidence of success. Plunging professors into foreign teaching situations without first giving them guides, maps, and adequate rations, while not as sinister a recommendation as one might think—faculty, like people, are an adaptable lot—is not always fruitful. In the first place, some people are reluctant to try it again. In the second place, word gets around and the next person you wanted to take the plunge says No. In the third place, some students dislike seeing their professors fidget.

support for adventure

The process of curricular change would be more productive with an effective system of support for faculty who want to try new things—if before and during the new course or program the professor works closely with persons knowledgeable about student and adult development. If the support system works, the number of faculty willing to climb out of old ruts is likely to increase.

Part of the plan already exists—the personnel. On hundreds of campuses, invisible as well as visible, faculty have created imaginative new programs. Their creators may not always know what works best, but they know what fails, and they know what failure does to the participants.

The other part of the plan, the supporting system, is another story. In most cases, no formal provisions have been made. In his report on the Project to Improve College Teaching, Kenneth Eble writes: "The need to establish adequate career development systems within institutions cannot be too strongly emphasized. . . . Faculty members from 142 different institutions were almost unanimous in responding negatively to the . . . question, 'My institution (does, does not) have an effective faculty development system' " (1972, p. 110). And H. Bradley Sagan observes, "among formal institutions, higher education institutions are perhaps the worst offenders in failing to provide for inservice development of staff" (1972, p. 23).

"We muddle through," most faculty say, when asked how they manage novel curricular adventures. "The administration says it wants us to do new things, but apart from moral support, we don't get much help." Moral support is important, but it is not enough. Nor is the periodic homily. Many college faculties, for example, begin the year by listening to a visiting luminary lecture on the importance of not lecturing and are later cajoled into hearing others say much the same thing. Now and then someone slides a copy of *Change* under their door or stuffs their mailbox with a bibliography on college teaching. But these efforts are usually unsystematic, unimaginative, and unproductive.

For one thing, no attempt is made to connect the panacea with the problem. It is as risky to generalize about the faculty's teaching problems as it is to generalize about the students' learning problems. What troubles one person may not trouble his colleague. Faculty are as wary of simplistic solutions as are students, and equally unlikely to be interested in learning what seems unrelated to their needs. What is required is systematic support for increasing the learning/teaching repertoire of faculty: special attention and help with personal and professional growth while they plan, teach, and evaluate new courses and programs.

benefits of interaction

I recently completed a study of an interdisciplinary faculty development program run by the Regional Council for International Education that contained elements of this systematic support. Four times a year, delegates from twenty-five colleges and universities lived together for forty-eight hours, listened to outstanding lectures delivered by outstanding scholars, and discussed their common interests at great length. The programs aimed to give participants current information on international developments, such as Revolution in Latin America one year or the Black African and Black American another.

The study of the program, sponsored by the Buhl Foundation, required us to conduct in-depth interviews with the two dozen participants. We were interested in more than the carry-over of content from the meetings. We wanted to learn something about the shoptalk of teaching and learning—how much of it took place, under what circumstances, and whether it led to actual changes in teaching attitudes and behavior.

The participants reported learning a great deal from the meetings, but we were struck during the interviews by their warm memories of the periods available for informal conversation—during meals, at the social hour before dinner, at night in the cabins—when many made new friends and found other people with the same teaching problems to talk with. The level of campus dialogue on teaching was reported to be superficial, yet the participants were obviously serious about their teaching. We concluded that this regional program was valuable not only because it gave participants more information on the announced topic but because it gave them an opportunity to share their burdens and triumphs with sympathetic and understanding acquaintances.

The same phenomenon can be observed in other interinstitutional programs. The Danforth Foundation's Workshops on Liberal Arts Education are valuable both because they introduce the institutional teams to distinguished consultants and because they introduce the teams to each other. For three weeks, a hundred front-line educators can indulge in endless shoptalk, and when they leave they take along a wealth of new ideas and contacts.

People who generalize glibly about professors' unconcern for their teaching have probably not talked in depth with many of them. The eagerness of our subjects to discuss their teaching with us was impressive, despite the number of them who could not recall reading recently any book or article on learning or teaching. The task, then, is to create a climate that encourages a free exchange of thoughts and experiences about teaching between institutions—one that supports the people in them. Could not groups of colleges create this environment, not just for three weeks during the summer, but on a continuing basis? Summer programs do not provide support for faculty initiative when the participants are back home trying out what they planned. But colleges within fairly easy driving distance of an attractive meeting place ought to be able to hold sessions there several times a year, and a program that combined summer workshops with day-long or weekend sessions during the year would be ideal.

beginning with the interested

Which faculty members should be involved in the program? Ask anyone who is teaching in an innovative course to assess himself as a teacher and you will probably hear a searching, troubled response. Such a person is more likely to benefit from a faculty development program than colleagues whose equilibrium has not been tampered with.

The faculty development model proposed here is designed to serve the needs of such risk-takers and to make them more able to assist colleagues who are trying new things. It rests on several simple assumptions: (1) If key faculty in innovative programs know more about student and faculty development, their programs will not only benefit students more but can be the vehicle for helping the development of other faculty. (2) Consortia can be as valuable for faculty learning as they are for student learning and institutional economy. (3) Faculty can learn as much from their counterparts in neighboring institutions as their students can learn from them. (4) Faculty are more likely to be open to advice and criticism in some areas from an extern than from a campus colleague. (5) The usefulness of advice does not depend on the donor's visibility but on his vision and firsthand experience.

Some improvements based on these premises can be made without a systematic plan of support. Even haphazard contacts among faculty from neighboring institutions are preferable to none. But the need for faculty development is so urgent that a systematic approach is called for.

The first step, then, is to identify a half-dozen or so persons who occupy leadership positions in your institution's curricular experiments: chairpersons of interdisciplinary staffs, directors of cluster colleges, certain department heads or innovative teachers, as examples. The selection is important, because unless these people enjoy the respect of their colleagues, the plan will fail.

resources nobody knows

Next, these individuals should assemble a detailed inventory of institutional resources in the areas of learning and teaching. Although the focus should be on human resources, other kinds should not be ignored. Here are some questions that might be answered by this inventory:

1. Who are your best lecturers?
2. Which faculty members run the best class discussions?
3. Who is most experienced with group learning projects?
4. Who is most experienced with independent learning projects?

5. Who knows how to use the community as an educational laboratory?

6. Who knows the most about sensitivity training?

7. Who uses role-playing effectively?

8. Who uses videotape most effectively?

9. Who teaches slow students the best?

10. Who does the best work with the brightest students?

11. Who is best at helping students improve their self-concept?

12. Who has experience in team-teaching?

13. Who has experience in interdisciplinary teaching?

14. Who teaches the best science courses for nonmajors?

15. Who knows how to run a film course?

16. Who has gone camping with students?

17. Who writes the best learning objectives?

18. Who knows most about the impact of dorm life on residents?

19. Who has the most coherent philosophy of education?

20. Who knows most about using the computer in courses?

21. Who knows most about testing and measurement of learning?

22. Who knows techniques for evaluating teaching?

23. Who knows most about student development?

24. Who knows most about adult development?

25. Who has written successful funding proposals? What for?

26. Who knows how to write proposals for experimental programs in a way that faculty will take seriously?

27. Who knows how to evaluate experimental programs?

28. Who are the best interviewers within the faculty?

29. Who knows how to run conferences?

30. What conference facilities do you have?

31. What measures of teaching effectiveness are used at your college? By whom?

32. What books and periodicals dealing with learning, teaching, and higher education are in your library? How do faculty know about their presence?

33. What reports are available on your new programs and courses? Who wrote them?

34. What reward system is used at your college to encourage faculty to try new things? Who thought it up?

35. What other resources does the college have for faculty development of which many faculty may not be aware?

This list is clearly incomplete, but it will serve to get things started. Colleges and universities are teeming with human resources, but almost no one realizes it. Professors, like prophets, are unhonored at home. This inventory, collated and distributed to the faculty and other interested persons, is not a difficult or expensive task but will probably trigger a long overdue exercise in consciousness-raising.

getting together

Next, contact must be established between the half-dozen or so leaders in innovation on your campus with their counterparts in neighboring colleges (defined as any institutions close enough to send delegates to a joint meeting who could come and get back the same day). An obvious place to begin is with the other members of a consortium, if your institution belongs to one. Since private colleges have a habit of consorting with other private institutions, it would be a good idea to build bridges with programs in one or two nearby state-supported institutions. The need for faculty development presses equally on both types. Ideally the mix should include institutions of all sorts, public and private, large and small, the invisible as well as the visible. The richer the mix, the richer the exchange.

At this point, all the delegates from all the institutions should meet each other, preferably in an attractive, informal, and neutral setting. In the model I am outlining, the first session should be at least two days long, and strangers, not colleagues, should be housed together. The participating institutions should pay all the costs, including the first night's open bar, as a token of gratitude for years of hard work and frustration.

Although delegates will have a considerable pool of collective wisdom in learning and teaching among themselves, I recommend that someone from outside the participating institutions who knows some things they may not know, for example, about developmental education and interinstitutional cooperation, be invited to attend and address this first meeting. He might even be asked to conduct it. One characteristic neighboring institutions frequently share is a conviction that their alleged excellence will somehow be compromised if they have too much to do with neighbors whose excellence they are inclined to question. The illusion of uniqueness often prevents serious interchange, something more than monthly meetings of deans and periodic intercollegiate games. Some of the resulting jealousies may be avoided if a respected outsider is entrusted with leadership of this meeting.

Two goals should be met during this initial get-together. First, individual faculty need to meet other faculty who are doing similar things; and a few workshop sessions on a range of experiments and opportunities for comparing notes will handle this. Second, the total group ought to agree on a strategy for continuing to use their energies, choosing from a variety of possibilities ranging from the highly informal "we'll-call-you-later" plan to the more structured "let's-elect-a-president-and-board" option. My model incorporates both.

Out of this initial assembly should come an agenda of short-range and long-range activities. Some short-term possibilities are:

1. Encourage the other colleges to utilize your colleagues who are listed in the resources inventory.

2. Invite a participant from another campus to sit in on a few of your classes and then tell you what he saw.

3. Invite someone from another college to teach a class session or a course at your college; teach a class there.

4. Invite several participants from other campuses to discuss their educational philosophies and experiments with you and other members of your faculty.

5. Schedule a course-planning session so someone from another college can participate.

6. Share reports on your experimental programs with the other participants and ask them to comment on them.

7. Together with the rest of your team, discuss with the dean and president changes in your institution that will help students and faculty develop more fully.

8. Ask your own colleagues to tell you about their teaching; practice listening.

9. Draft a proposal asking a local foundation to underwrite the costs of continuing the interinstitutional meetings.

Some long-range activities, set up with the other institutional teams, might be:

1. An ongoing workshop in learning and teaching that will expand teaching repertoires.

2. A training program to raise the self awareness level of par
ticipants.

3. Sessions to teach participants to be effective interviewers,
so they can assist other faculty to be more self-aware.

4. Sessions on student and adult development, so participants
can be more effective teachers and catalysts for faculty development.

5. A laboratory in course and program design, with a hefty
component on evaluation.

6. A seminar on the evaluation of teaching.

7. Demonstrations on using the local community as a learning
resource.

8. A seminar on change and how to help colleagues survive it
and thrive as a result.

9. An introduction to the literature on students, teaching,
and the history of higher education.

Again, the list is incomplete, and it would be unwise to try to
implement many such projects in one year. In fact, the first ones
attempted should be those with a high probability of success: it is
important to begin by winning since winning builds more trust than
losing.

implementation

Implementing the long-range goals requires more shrewdness
and hard-nosed planning than the first activities, and here the tal-
ents of externs may be needed. Raising the level of self-awareness
among participating faculty, for instance, is no easy task. Many
professors will admit that, as a class, faculty are probably not more
aware of why they do what they do than any other group, and that
their future development presupposes habits of reflection and an
openness to new experiences. Nor will many disagree that just as
knowledge about student development is an important prelude to
helping them learn better, knowledge about adult development, and
especially the maturation of professors, makes it easier to understand themselves and work together. But where do you go from
there? How do you acquire that knowledge?

My recommendation is that the interinstitutional groups
work closely with the best people on faculty development they can
find elsewhere. If the member colleges lack experience, they should
import, not improvise. Through a weekend workshop, periodic

meetings, or even a summer institute, such resource persons can prepare the six-person delegations to become more effective agents of faculty development. The better the program, the better the product.

The length and organization of these sessions will depend largely on the concerns of participants and their institutions, reflected in the agendas drawn up at the initial meeting. It is reasonable to assume, however, that a summer institute of several weeks' duration might be a better setting for raising the self-awareness level of participants than a weekend workshop, while a seminar on evaluation, change, or the history of American education could probably be handled well if it were spread out over several months. A summer session is probably best designed to help faculty learn new ideas and techniques; then follow-up sessions can give them a chance to compare notes with other participants who are busy putting the summer's inspirations into practice. If learning how to interview other faculty is a priority, for example, the summer workshop would be a good place to begin. But since interviewing back home will be different from doing it with other participants, some provision should be made that would allow the new interviewers to check their success against that of the group.

Whether these half-dozen retreaded educators will eventually be invited to invade the territories of their colleagues will no doubt depend on institutional folkways and individual feelings. College faculty members often build walls to keep their colleagues out of certain compartments of their lives. While many of them might agree, for example, that inviting peers into their courses would be one way to get valuable feedback on teaching, few are doing it. The reason probably has less to do with the sacredness of the classroom than with the sacredness of the psyche. It is bad enough to feel inadequate about teaching, as many professors do, without proving it to the person in the next office. One advantage of an interinstitutional approach is that it automatically creates an alternative source of consulting talent. If colleagues will not let you in, they might admit your counterpart from a neighboring college.

The whole point of these recommendations is to create within institutions a critical mass of faculty who not only understand learning and teaching, and do both well, but who also know how to help other colleagues to develop. Leaders of experimental courses and programs seem to be the natural people to begin the process.

The model of interinstitutional communication I have presented provides the necessary faculty support system—too many programs have none. If, every year, six new persons from an institution participate in such a faculty development program, the college should be further along the road to renewal in three or four years. And its relationship with neighboring colleges and universities should be much more vital as a result.

references

Eble, K. E. *Professors As Teachers.* San Francisco: Jossey-Bass, 1972.
Noonan, J. F. "The Impact of Curricular Change on Faculty Behavior." *Liberal Education,* 1971, *57,* 344-358.
Noonan, J. F. "Curricular Change: A Strategy for Improving Teaching." In D. W. Vermilye (Ed.), *The Expanded Campus: Current Issues in Higher Education 1972.* San Francisco: Jossey-Bass, 1972.
Sagan, H. B. "Organizational Reform Is Not Enough." In C. U. Walker (Ed.), *Elements Involved in Academic Change.* Washington, D. C.: Association of American Colleges, 1972.

John Noonan is associate professor of English and chairman of the Liberal Studies Program at Findlay College. The Liberal Studies Program is an interdisciplinary, problem-oriented, core program for all Findlay students, in which some twenty faculty members participate each year. Professor Noonan is serving as an advisor to several institutions, consortia, and agencies on faculty development and the management of innovation and has drafted a plan for "Facilitating Faculty and Student Development through Interinstitutional Cooperation" which develops his model in greater detail and is available from him at Findlay College, Findlay, Ohio 45840.

Interviews with faculty can stimulate
their self-awareness and form the
basis of a development program.

facilitating faculty development

mervin freedman

The two preceding articles present examples and models of faculty development programs. Here I want to supplement those presentations by describing how interviews with professors can form the basis of a faculty development effort.

interviewing faculty members

An interview is an excellent procedure—probably the very best procedure—for stimulating faculty members to reflect on their own development and on their institutional situation. I refer to a comprehensive interview which contains such questions as:

- What are the circumstances that led to your accepting a position at this college or university?
- Would you prefer to have an appointment at a different institution, and, if so, for what reasons?
- What were the good and bad points of your undergraduate education? Your graduate education?
- How would you describe your philosophy of education?

105

• Do you think that students have changed in the past several years? If so, in what ways?

• What are the rewards of teaching graduate students? Undergraduate students? What are the problems?

It has been our experience that faculty members almost universally enjoy talking about such matters. In the majority of cases they are disposed to go on talking about them long beyond the scheduled end of the interview. And certainly it is surprising but not uncommon to hear a faculty member say "I have never thought about this before."

A penetrating interview that captures the imagination and focuses attention and concern on one's personal and professional development, on matters of teaching, on institutional workings, and on individual hopes and goals is the first step in heightening self-awareness and broadening perspective. These interviews can be conducted either by an outsider, such as an interested and congenial faculty member from a neighboring institution (as Noonan proposes earlier in this issue) or a special consultant, or by faculty members from within the institution. The important thing is that the interviewers not be involved with those being interviewed in some consequential way—for example, in friendship or a power relationship—which would inhibit free exchange in the interview. These criteria tend to rule out inside interviewers on small campuses. If a significant proportion—a "critical mass"—of the professors in a department, school, or college are interviewed, they are likely to discuss the interviews with one another and thereby establish an atmosphere in which the issues of the interview become matters of conversation and widespread interest.

discussing the results

Interviews and informal conversations alone, however, are not enough to make a significant difference in the lives of faculty members—or in the workings of their colleges. If we intend that faculty should provide substantial educational leadership, something more is needed. Institutional change may depend on personal change to a considerable degree, but personal change by itself is not likely to produce institutional change.

Kurt Lewin (1948) has explicated how changes in attitude and values require social support, the reinforcement of "significant others." Students, for example, require significant others—faculty members and fellow students—in order to learn effectively; books or libraries are not sufficient. Similarly, consequential change among faculty members depends on their interactions with important figures, some of whom may be students or administrators but surely are other faculty. Thus the next step in building this social support structure is systematic discussion of the interview results with the interviewed professors as a group. The data collected from the interviews must be analyzed as rigorously and quantitatively as possible by the interviewer-researcher, but a freely interpretive report to the participants is in order as well. Then opportunities must be provided for faculty to discuss the findings. Some of these discussion sessions probably should be limited in size to groups small enough for intimate exchange—ten members, possibly—although for some purposes larger groups may be preferable. These reports and discussions should recur over a period of time. One or several sessions are likely to have little lasting impact, but distributed over a semester or a year, their influence can be cumulative.

I am not suggesting group experiences of an encounter or semitherapy kind—that is, procedures directed primarily at *personal* growth—although such experiences may be valuable. I have in mind discussions that center on educational issues and at the same time provide ample opportunity for personal reflection and response. I suggest, in fact, that some of the meetings center on didactic presentations—discussions of student development, personality development in the adult years, or problem-centered versus discipline-centered approaches to teaching, for example—in addition to the interview findings.

taking action

Meetings of this kind will surely generate interesting ideas and experiences that contribute to heightened self-awareness and expanded perspective on the world. But ideas and awareness by themselves are insufficient; they must be coupled with action. The days of getting by on fine rhetoric in higher education are past. Faculty need to take responsible action designed to promote their own development and that of their students. With few exceptions, faculty suffer a paralysis of nerve. In the face of criticism, financial retrenchment, and demands for accountability they retreat into attempts to preserve whatever privileges and prerogatives they now possess. Ideas, no matter how good, must eventuate in action or they will die aborning.

I stress action, responsible action, because higher education in the true liberal sense is being squeezed in a vise between unthinking conformity to the status quo and millenarian visions unattached to mechanisms by which these utopian goals may be realized. There is but one way to achieve the noble goals of higher education, as they are expounded in all the college and university catalogs in the land. It is to delineate the steps by which these goals are to be realized, to assess progress toward the goals, and then to readjust means and goals as changing circumstances dictate. Not a glamorous or dramatic way of proceeding, perhaps, but the alternatives are the tyrannies of mindless conservatism or ideological overkill. The history of science demonstrates that good general theory has not emerged from deliberate attempts to produce it. Rather it has emerged out of the constant interplay between imagination and empirical observation. The best educational theory and the best educational policies will develop in the same way—by taking planned action, by assessing its effects in the light of experience, and by revising actions as necessary.

Interviews and their discussion can lead to developing a theory of higher education as a system—relating theories of faculty and student development to theories of how colleges and universities function as social systems. Out of such discussions may emerge programs of action directed at any or all of these critical needs in higher education:

(1) Clarifying individual and institutional rights and responsibilities, based on refined conceptions of the individual and the community, one of the most urgent demands of our time.

(2) Experimenting with ways to organize knowledge different from those of current departments. A curriculum centered on problems and issues rather than disciplines is one alternative—for example, the origins of war, urban problems, seventeenth-century Britain.

(3) Revising curricula by integrating the concept of student development with the intellectual goals and activities of colleges and universities. Too often concern with student development is interpreted to mean that faculty members should eschew their intellectual or disciplinary concerns and become counselors or psycho-

therapists. Consequently, faculty members avoid examining the goals of student development and finding ways to meet them. The proper intellectual and educational issue, however, is how to promote student development by means of the curriculum (Axelrod and others, 1969).

(4) Experimenting with various ways to assess field work, independent study, colleges and universities without walls, and similar departures from the traditional classroom or lecture hall.

(5) Relating the professional roles and functions of professors to information about personality development in adults (Erikson, 1959, 1963; Levinson, 1972; Livson, in press; Neugarten, 1968; Reichard and others, 1962).

(6) Developing good teachers by revising graduate education with this goal in mind and learning how to identify good teachers and reward them.

The educational researchers and consultants of the Wright Institute have engaged in action-oriented programs of faculty development of the kind discussed here often enough to know that they yield useful results. This is not to say, of course, that all faculty members or even a majority are interested in participating. Many are wary, even negative. But there is no need for all faculty on any campus to be involved in development programs, as long as those participating represent a sufficient minority (at least a quarter, probably) to form a critical mass within the institution or certain of its subsystems. If something worthwhile is going on, faculty who are not interested at first will be influenced by contagion. They will participate actively later, or they may be affected in somewhat less direct fashion by observing participants or by conversations with them.

aiding the process

I do not mean to suggest even for one minute that carrying out an effective, action-oriented development program is easy, given the complexity of human nature and social institutions. Competition between individuals and between departments or schools, struggles for power and dominance, disposition to rebel compulsively against authority of any kind, behavior of individuals that may be termed psychopathological—these and other influences are likely to impede the work of those who are trying to experiment and grow. For this reason the services of one or several individuals who are skilled in interpreting and managing group complexities are a necessity. Without such help, programs designed to facilitate professional growth and to foster educational leadership on the part of faculty are likely to founder. I am inclined to say that lack of such special aid is the chief reason why so many well-laid innovative plans slowly disintegrate or abruptly stop. High intelligence and high levels of cognitive functioning in research and disciplinary activities are no barrier against the contrary emotional forces that prevent social groups from carrying out their assigned tasks (Bion, 1959; Miller and Rice, 1967; Rioch, 1971).

Some of these skilled individuals will be found among indigenous faculty leaders. A special member of the institution, such as a faculty development officer who is neither an administrator (in the sense of holding power over individual faculty members) nor only a member of the faculty (in the sense of being a colleague of particular faculty members) can play this role, as can an outside consultant. The interpretation of group behavior requires the presence of a figure who can and does stand outside the group but not above it. Administrators, department chairmen, and comparable figures who stand in a relationship of power or authority to faculty members cannot serve in such capacities, since development programs must proceed in so far as possible free of the fetters of concern for pleasing or offending established authority.

a time for help

Hefferlin (1969) describes how the initiative for academic reform historically has come from outside colleges and universities, or outside their faculty—from students, from the needs of farms and industry, from political officers, from the pressures of society. He explicates the complexities and difficulties that have almost totally barred reform from within. Although one can hardly be sanguine that things are different now, they may be changing. It may be that the situation, at least in some colleges and universities, is coming to resemble the New England town as it was prior to mass migration—a situation in which people knew they were going to be living together for a lifetime and had to make the accommodations necessary to assure maximum privilege and freedom for all. In the face of reduced faculty mobility, fewer financial resources, and a general public disposition to cast a skeptical eye on higher education, perhaps faculty members can produce communities among themselves that provide maximal opportunity for the exercise of educational leadership as well as for their own development and that of students.

references

Axelrod, J., Freedman, M., Hatch, W., Katz, J., and Sanford, N. *Search for Relevance.* San Francisco: Jossey-Bass, 1969.

Bion, W. R. *Experiences in Groups.* New York: Basic Books, 1959.

Erikson, E. "Identity and the Life Cycle." In *Psychological Issues.* New York: International Universities Press, 1959.

Erikson, E. *Childhood and Society.* 2nd ed. New York: Norton, 1963.

Hefferlin, JB L. *The Dynamics of Academic Reform.* San Francisco: Jossey-Bass, 1969.

Levinson, D. J., and Associates. "Personality Development in Adult Men." New Haven: Yale University, 1972 (mimeographed).

Lewin, K. *Resolving Social Conflicts: Selected Papers on Group Dynamics.* G. W. Lewin (Ed.) New York: Harper and Row, 1948.

Livson, N. "Developmental Dimensions of Personality: A Life-Span Formulation." In *Life-Span Developmental Psychology: Personality and Socialization.* New York: Academic Press (in press).

Miller, E. J., and Rice, A. K. *Systems of Organization.* London: Tavistock, 1967.

Neugarten, B. L. (Ed.) *Middle Age and Aging.* Chicago: University of Chicago Press, 1968.

Reichard, S., Livson, F., and Peterson, P. G. *Aging and Personality.* New York: Wiley, 1962.

Rioch, M. J. " 'All We Like Sheep.' (Isaiah 53:6): Followers and Leaders." *Psychiatry,* 1971, *34,* 258-273.

*Background on other publications
bearing on the problem of
faculty growth and development.*

additional resources

norbert ralph
mervin freedman

No associations or agencies as yet specialize in helping create faculty development programs of the type described in this sourcebook—nor to the best of our knowledge do any of the consulting firms active in higher education. Among the authors of the following materials, however, are individuals who may be of assistance to an institution working on the problem.

This annotated bibliography of books and articles is not intended to be exhaustive but rather to serve as a point of departure. For those who want more extensive sources, we suggest *The World of Higher Education* by Paul Dressel and Sally Pratt. San Francisco: Jossey-Bass, 1971.

Brawer, Florence B. *Personality Characteristics of College and University Faculty: Implications for the Community College.* ERIC Clearinghouse for Junior College Information, AAJC monograph series. Washington, D. C.: American Association of Junior Colleges, 1968.

One of the best summaries of sociological and psychological research on college faculty. The areas covered are the general characteristics of college teachers, faculty types, faculty selection, teacher training, innovation, and student-teacher interactions. Like most eclectic summaries, it seems a bit disjointed, at times. One may, of course, consult the primary sources if more detailed information is needed.

Brown, J. W., and Shukraft, R. C. "Personality Development and Professional Practice in College and University Professors." Unpublished doctoral dissertation. Berkeley: Graduate Theological Union, 1971.

The research project described in this joint Ph.D. dissertation is the basis for much of the empirical work described in this issue of *New Directions for Higher Education.* It provides useful additions to the ethonography of faculty cultures. Several chapters also explicate faculty development in relation to theories of personality development in adults. The dissertation contains an extensive bibliography.

Clark, Burton R. "Faculty Culture." In *The Study of Campus Cultures.* Berkeley: Western Interstate Commission for Higher Education and Center for the Study of Higher Education, 1962.

In this article Clark undertakes a sociological analysis of faculty culture. He presents a four-fold typology of faculty orientations and determinants of these sociological types. He also discusses trends which point to increased pressure toward cosmopolitan and professional orientations in faculty. A thoughtful analysis.

Cottle, Thomas J. "The Pains of Permanence." In Bardwell L. Smith (Ed.), *The Tenure Debate.* San Francisco: Jossey-Bass, 1973.

Well-known to readers of *Change* magazine, Cottle here evokes the feelings of a young academic from the time he moves into his Harvard office as an assistant professor until he leaves for another university just before the time that he expects, like most other junior faculty at Harvard, to be told he has not been given tenure. The young academic is Cottle himself, and the account is ironic, even shameless. In short, it openly describes the fantasies, fears, and jealousies that hardly any academic has a chance to discuss, even if he (or she) becomes conscious of them; and it likewise charts some strategems and rationalizations developed in the quest for tenure and in the denial of that quest. Since academics watch the struggle for promotion and mobility as avidly as others cheer quarterbacks or bet on horses, Cottle's revelations, like some recent autobiographies of sporting heroes, will be greeted with dismay and no little curiosity. Apart from novelists, Cottle is among the few writers who, negotiating their authenticity, take us behind the official face of the academic world.

Eble, Kenneth E. "The Recognition and Evaluation of Teaching" and "Career Development of the Effective College Teacher." Reports of The Project to Improve College Teaching. Washington, D. C.: The Association of American Colleges and the American Association of University Professors, 1971; *Professors as Teachers.* San Francisco: Jossey-Bass, 1972.

Sponsored by two national associations, funded for two years by the Carnegie Corporation, advised by a distinguished board, The Project to Improve College Teaching searched the "literature," visited a wide variety of campuses, circulated a questionnaire, and held a number of regional conferences. The purpose of this activity was to "study the recognition and evaluation of teaching, the career development of effective college teachers, and the development of optimum working conditions for effective teaching." Many of the recommendations are useful, but the study is vitiated by its blandness. Eble writes as follows, for example: "I cannot say that my visits of the past two years have made me join those, like Paul Dressel, who locate many of the ills of the university in the departmental structure. Yet, I respect that position, for one cannot work very long in the university without becoming aware of the baneful influence of the department." What should be done? Well, in this case, the department should simply be subverted by its chairman! Eble does not say why a chairman would be motivated to try this or how he could go about it. As a well-intentioned and practical guide to the reforms possible in teaching without seriously altering any of the basic relationships within higher education, these writings deserve close study.

Evans, Richard I. *Resistance to Innovation in Higher Education.* San Francisco: Jossey-Bass, 1967.

An intensive study of an attempt to implement an innovative teaching technique, instructional television, in a metropolitan university. The author addresses the general issue of resistance to and diffusion of educational innovation. The theoretical and methodological sophistication of the work is unique in this area. Since the primary target group for innovation is university faculty, the book is highly relevant reading for those wishing to undertake programs of faculty development. The author's method-centered approach sometimes prevents the reader from seeing the real significance of his research.

Light, Donald W., Jr. "The Structure of the Academic Professions." Introductory essay by the editor of a forthcoming issue of *Sociology of Education*.

Most striking in this generally useful essay is Light's sharp critique of the description of the academic profession as put forth by Talcott Parsons and Gerald Platt. So far a draft of their material has circulated in mimeograph form and fragments have appeared in a number of journals; when published as a whole, it will undoubtedly have a wide influence, if only because of the status of its senior author. Light argues, however, that the work by Parsons and Platt, far from being a neutral description, is an ideological defense of a certain set of elitist universities, and that to this end the authors draw misleading conclusions even from their own survey data. For example, the data are said to demonstrate faculty concern for teaching, an assertion that presumably rebuffs critics of undergraduate education; yet, as Light shows, what the respondents in fact say is that they want to spend more time with disciplinary apprentices, not with college students. Elsewhere, Light extends Alvin Gouldner's well-known distinction between locals and cosmopolitans on the faculty, rearranges a typology of institutions proposed by Fulton and Trow, and proposes a distinction among disciplinary scholars (whoever employs them), holders of academic appointments (regardless of whether they are productive in a discipline), and the intersection of these two categories, namely, research-oriented academics. He also insists on the obvious but widely neglected point that academics are professionals not in their teaching but only in their various disciplines; contrary to most writers, he asserts that no academic profession, as such, exists. To judge by Light's introduction, this whole issue of *Sociology of Education* will be valuable.

Mann, Richard D. *The College Classroom: Conflict, Change and Learning*. New York: Wiley, 1970.

This is the most intensive and insightful work written on classroom interaction. It analyzes the natural history of four discussion sections and examines how feelings and affects can be constructive or disruptive to the task of classroom learning. The book shows that the mundane and seemingly insignificant give and take of classroom interaction is in fact highly significant and critical in achieving the primary task of a course. The author holds that no one style of teaching or classroom procedure is most effective; a style of teaching that is successful at the beginning of a term may fall flat later on. The work has profound implications for college teaching.

Morimoto, Kiyo. "Supervising Teachers in Groups." Cambridge: Bureau of Study Counsel, Harvard University, 1970 (mimeographed).

This paper provides an excellent model for training college professors as teachers. Tape recordings of actual classroom interactions serve as a basis for discussions with graduate student teaching assistants. In the relaxed climate of these groups graduate students are able to consider a range of alternatives in teaching behavior and begin to develop their own individual styles. A word of caution: implementation of this approach to teaching is subject to the same types of manipulative, shallow, or faddish applications that have plagued T-groups or sensitivity groups. Individuals who assume leadership of such activities should have adequate training or supervision.

Perry, William G., Jr. *Forms of Intellectual and Ethical Development in the College Years: A Scheme.* New York: Holt, Rinehart and Winston, 1970.

This is the most original work on personality development of college students to appear since the field was founded twenty years ago. The book outlines a series of stages which describe the evolution of the forms of students' epistemological assumptions about the nature of knowledge and values. The scheme traces a transition from simple dualistic world views, which divide the world into good and bad by some authority, to viewpoints where commitment can be found within a relativistic field. The book is an intellectual effort of the first caliber and has major implications for the art of teaching.

Riesman, David. "The Academic Career: Notes on Recruitment and Colleagueship." *Daedalus*, 1959, *88*, 147-167; *The Academic Revolution* (with Christopher Jencks), Garden City, N.Y.: Doubleday, 1968, especially Chapter Twelve, "Reforming the Graduate Schools"; *Academic Values and Mass Education* (with Joseph Gusfield and Zelma Gamson), Garden City, N.Y.: Doubleday, 1970, especially Chapters Four through Nine; "An Academic Great Depression?" *University Quarterly*, Winter 1971, *26:1*, 15-27; and "Notes on Educational Reform," *The Journal of General Education*, 1971, *23:2*, 81-110.

Drolly observant, broadly informed and sinuous, playing with received wisdom, including his own, like a cat with yarn, Riesman displays the tensions that shape academic life and are missed by single-minded writers. As is evident from the date of the first of these papers, Riesman has long been working up an ethnography of higher education, and these samples from his steady output provide a rich context for any consideration of faculty development. Here a reader can find many elements of the academic life cycle: recruitment, graduate training, colleagueship, efforts at educational reform, a variety of settings, eroded expectations. A complement to the primarily psychological studies done at the Wright Institute, Riesman's sociological and historical insights go to both the need for and the vagaries of academic reform. Some readers mistrust his thought because, like the flight of a wasp or a butterfly, it is hard to take notes on; they want to pin him down to a position. For many other readers, however, Riesman provides the most substantial and suggestive ethnography we have in this field.

Rothwell, C. Easton. *The Importance of Teaching: A Memorandum to the New College Teacher*. New Haven: The Hazen Foundation, undated.

A good pamphlet for the beginning teacher, offering useful suggestions in a number of areas including choice of institution, teaching procedures and strategies, evaluation, and the ideal teaching environment. The suggestions on teaching strategies lack the complexity of Mann's book, but overall the pamphlet is a good resource.

Sanford, Nevitt (Ed.). *The American College: A Psychological and Social Interpretation of the Higher Learning*. New York: Wiley, 1962.

This collection of twenty-nine essays is one of the classic works on American higher education. A wide range of issues is explored. The essays most relevant to faculty development are Robert Knapp's "The Changing Functions of the College Professor," W. J. McKeachie's "Procedures and Techniques of Teaching: a Survey of Experimental Studies," and Joseph Adelson's "The Teacher as Model."

Sofer, Cyril. *The Organization from Within: A Comparative Study of Social Institutions Based on a Sociotherapeutic Approach.* London: Tavistock Publications, 1961.

Sofer, an organizational consultant, presents three case histories of organizations, one of which is an analysis of a program of faculty development. He provides an excellent description of the complexity and vicissitudes of such programs, as well as appropriate strategies for their conduct. A good text for individuals concerned with consultation in higher education.

Veysey, Laurence R. *The Emergence of the American University.* Chicago: University of Chicago Press, 1965. Also available as a Phoenix paperback.

At a time when "futurologists" distract us with new charts following the failure of unruly events to conform to their last set of predictions, one hesitates before recommending a history of old-fashioned developments between 1865 and 1910. Yet Veysey's book, unlike futurology in education or elsewhere, has the density of life as we know it. It is useful both to those who imagine the American university was created in its ideal form just before they became aware of it and to others who, feeling the pain and waste in this institution, imagine that if only they were in power they could change it with one stroke. Alert not only to the themes thickly tangled in the development of American universities, but also to the "silences" that suggest what could no longer or not yet be said by aspiring academics, Veysey thinks with a vigor and complexity that put most current books on higher education to shame. His remarkable display of political sense offers as much reward to the reader as his agility in following cultural developments.

index